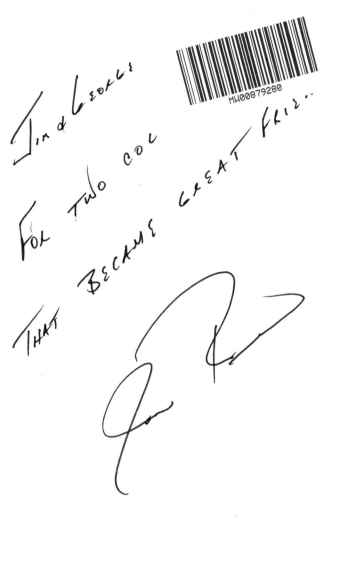

Jim & George,

For two cops
that became great frie...

DON'T LET THE BASTARDS BEAT YOU!

ALL ABOUT STALKING
by

Joseph E. Rice

authorHOUSE

1663 LIBERTY DRIVE, SUITE 200
BLOOMINGTON, INDIANA 47403
(800) 839-8640
www.authorhouse.com

First published by AuthorHouse 08/02/04

ISBN: 1-4184-2039-5 (e)
ISBN: 1-4184-2038-7 (sc)

Library of Congress Control Number: 2004096101

Printed in the United States of America
Bloomington, Indiana

This book is printed on acid-free paper.

REMEMBERING MOM

Since the beginning of the creation of this book, my mother passed away. Unfortunately, she did not see a published copy of this book, however she was able to inspect one of the final drafts of the manuscript. Other than the fact that she scolded me over the choice of a title, which she made clear that she did not like, she was proud of what I was trying to do.

Mom was an educator for forty-four years, teaching almost exclusively first grade. Her stock in trade was that she loved the "little ones" and she believed that without the ability to read, one was facing a long dark life.

A woman, small in stature, but a giant in character, she knew what she believed, she knew what she stood for, and she knew where she was going at the end of life's journey … and we all know she's there now, talking to the greats of history, and if there is such a need, teaching those to read who didn't learn while they were with us.

While this book is primarily dedicated to others, it could not go to press without mention of her influence on my life. The tragedy of so many young today that are growing up without strong parental influence is taking a serious toll on our society. I was fortunate in that I was blessed with two strong parents that shaped my beliefs long before I began my life's work.

My mother gave me the blessing of being able to communicate which has served me well throughout my entire life.

The theme of this book deals primarily with a crisis involving women today, crisis that is born of young men without values. What better place to honor her influence on my life.

Today we hear a great misuse of the word hero. A hero is simply defined as an ordinary person doing extraordinary things. I believe that a woman that lived 80 years, unwavering in her beliefs, was a faithful wife for fifty-eight years, raised a family, and taught thousands of children to read for forty-four years qualifies to be called a hero.

And so, as you read this, just remember that a tough dedicated school teacher passed judgment on my words, and thought them appropriate ... all except the title.

DEDICATION

This book is dedicated to one person and several select groups, all of whom have moved me over the years in the course of my various endeavors.

First of all, I want to dedicate this book to the memory of the "Old Man," our boss of so many years ago who instilled in us the courage to "stay the course" when others believed that the cause of peace and justice was impossible in the situations in which we had been placed ... having the responsibility of protecting those whom we had sworn to God to protect and the laws that we had sworn to God to uphold.

His style, his dedication, and his commitment, not only to his oath, but also to the task at hand, while never forgetting his commitment to those who he commanded, were the seeds that grew in young men, creating giant oaks of commitment to whatever cause in which they found themselves.

His simple, direct, "speak softly" style and, most of all, his simple but direct order to us that night so many years ago was typical of his style ... simple and direct ... words that have stayed with each of us for all these years and through numerous situations.

So, to the "Old Man," thanks ever so much. I would say that you didn't realize the strength of your words that night, but I would be wrong ... for you always knew exactly what you were saying.

And to all of those friends, family, and loved ones who have tirelessly listened to me on those occasions when I wished to opine on nearly every controversial subject that presented itself, thank you for your confidence and support. Though I'll always wonder if the frequently repeated suggestion that I should write a book was an attempt to ease the pain of listening to me, I shall choose to believe that it was sincere and express my gratitude.

And last, but certainly not the least, to all the victims, those that I have known, and those that I may never know. Some of you have suffered in the past, and some of you are suffering today … but the more I learn, the more I am touched by each of you. And so all of you share a portion of the dedication of these words … with the sincerest hope that you will find strength and guidance, and others will find knowledge of this most horrible form of abuse that only you can ever understand.

INTRODUCTION

Now, before I bring down the full force and wrath of the "Bible Belt" upon me over my choice of a title for this book, please allow me to explain myself.

Quite a few years ago, as a young state trooper, I was assigned to an institution in an undercover position, attempting to develop information that would, hopefully, avoid the tragedy that had occurred at that same institution just one year earlier. For reasons of controversy, I shall not go into detail over what the location was, but suffice to say that it had gained national attention and was surrounded with controversy.

While the annals of history may not reveal the seriousness of the threat and the danger to the public, from one who was there, I can tell you that the entire operation was surrounded with serious risk, not only to those of us who were assigned there, but also to the public.

I had been assigned there alone for several months, during which time I developed an information network for later use. At the appropriate time, a squad of operatives was sent to join me. We were in place for about two months preceding the anniversary of the tragedy.

We were assigned to a District Commander who was, in all my experience, the classiest guy under which I ever had the opportunity to serve. He was quiet and mild mannered, but when he spoke, there was no doubt who was in command.

We were in daily contact with him, providing the necessary information that allowed him to wade through the hierarchy of brass in our own organization, many of which had no real responsibility for the situation, but felt that they should "be in the loop" to serve their own needs … and at the same time keeping the politicians aware of the moment-by-moment moods of the insurgents and their sympathizers. Not the least of his responsibilities was that of dealing on a daily basis, 24/7, with a local official who was the one who would send out the call for uniform troops to enter the situation if things became volatile. His dealings with this individual not only required keeping him in check when he began to panic, but also keeping him sober. He had apparently been quite a drinker for a long time, but after the initial tragedy, he was out of control.

Our job was to provide information and read situations, forwarding information to the "boss" when needed to allow him to make the appropriate decisions. If a situation that was volatile but not yet violent were to have uniform troopers introduced before necessary, the opposite result of that which was intended was not only a distinct possibility, but also a distinct probability. The boss had a big job; he trusted and relied on us, and we weren't going to let him down.

Our routine those days was that of being in the appropriate places from early afternoon until almost dawn. This could be on the streets, in bars, in clandestine meetings, in possible explosive trouble spots, and anywhere else that could be necessary to immediately read what either was about to happen or was already happening. It was a twenty-four-hour/seven–day-a-week job.

About two weeks prior to the anniversary of the tragedy, the boss told us to block a Monday night and that he had a different assignment for the entire squad. He told us to bring our wives, girlfriends, or whomever; meet in another city, miles from where we worked; be there at a well-known nightclub at 7:00 PM; and that we were all having dinner, to be followed by an evening of entertainment.

It seems that the owner of the club was a lifetime friend of the boss, and he had made special arrangements. Mondays were the slowest time of the week for us, since all the bad guys that we were watching were resting after their weekend activities, but we knew that with one phone call, about ten wives and girlfriends would be finishing dinner and driving home alone.

The boss kept the entertainment secret until after dinner. We had a great evening relaxing without looking over our shoulders, and after we finished, we gave the boss a box of his favorite cigars, telling him how glad we were to be working for him. The boss thanked us and said that he had a few words of his own for us.

When he began to speak, it was in that same quiet, commanding tone that we had all grown to recognize ... sort of a Clint Eastwood style of speaking. He told us that he didn't want to be melodramatic and didn't want to upset wives and girlfriends in the group, but the fact remained that in the next few weeks things might begin to occur that could conceivably prohibit us from ever assembling in this same group together again—a fact of which we were all aware. He said that others may never know the extent of our efforts in the protection of others, but that he knew, and he wanted us to know that he would be forever grateful.

We, too, knew that others would never know what we had done, but if the "Old Man" knew, and he was satisfied, that was enough for us.

As he concluded his remarks, he told us to pick up a small dish that was in front of each of our place settings. We all did, and underneath each small plate was a business card with the words inscribed, "DON'T LET THE BASTARDS BEAT YOU!"

The boss told us to carry those cards with us, and someday after all this was over, possibly we would find someone else who might benefit from his brief directive. With that, he was done talking, in the true style to which we had become so accustomed.

I carried my card for many years and only surrendered it to a client of mine, a stalking victim, telling this story and giving the same instructions to her.

So, for those of you who may not like my choice of a title … get over it! It's an ugly world out there, and I'm sure those who may benefit from the message of this book won't mind … they may even think it appropriate.

By the way, the entertainment that night was Duke Ellington. It was the last year that he toured before he died, and we'd never experienced anything like the show that we saw that Monday night. He sat with us during each break, and all of us young, hard-nosed state troopers who thought we were tougher and knew more than anyone were shown something that we'd never experienced before.

I guess that's why we thought the "Old Man" was bigger than life, and that's why when he asked, we stood ready to do whatever needed done. And as you wander through this book—should you be reading in a search for answers or help—remember his command to us ... and "DON'T LET THE BASTARDS BEAT YOU!"

TABLE OF CONTENTS DON'T LET THE BASTARDS BEAT YOU!

.

Invictus

Out of the night that covers me,
Dark as the pit from pole to pole,
I thank whatever gods may be
For my unconquerable soul.

In the fell clutch of circumstance
I have not winced nor cried aloud,
Under the bludgeoning of chance
My head is bloody, but unbowed.

Beyond this place of wrath and tears
Looms but the horror of the shade,
And yet the menace of the years
Finds, and shall find me, unafraid.

It matters not how strait the gate,
How charged with punishments the scroll,
I am the master of my fate;
I am the captain of my soul.

—William Ernest Henley

CHAPTER 1
ALL ABOUT ME

Certainly there are those who would consider my choice of subjects for the first chapter of my book a blatant, arrogant attempt at self-promotion … and maybe so; however, the subject matter of this book deals with deeply personal, serious, and many times dangerous issues. Were I to be engaging a client involving these issues, the most immediate process would be that of the client and me developing a relationship with each other. That requires both parties to learn about each other.

Some of you who read this book will be doing so for purposes of general knowledge or just plain curiosity. And sadly but hopefully, there will be those of you who are reading these words in a search for answers to a personal crisis. For all of you curiosity seekers, I'm sure that you will want to know who this "joker" is that is espousing his philosophies, and for those of you seeking answers, it is imperative that you know with whom you are dealing.

There are others who have written on this subject, and the number of varying opinions is directly proportional to the number of authors on the subject. The information contained in the following pages represents the experience that I have gained from handling many of these cases. That knowledge is gained from personal experience with law enforcement, social agencies, psychologists, and, of most importance, those most affected, the victims.

Make no mistake; this is a societal problem that, while rare not so many years ago, has escalated with a frightening frequency.

I hope that my experiences will enlighten you, whatever your reason for reading ... so, let's learn "all about me."

I was born in a small town in the Midwest, the son of a carpenter and a school teacher. We were a religious family, which, in my formative years, caused me extreme constraint. It seemed that everything that I chose to do that was popular at the time was contrary to the teachings of the church. We were Protestant, and in those days, a "mixed" marriage was a Protestant and anybody else. Needless to say, I was a "Catholic magnet."

Of course, being the oldest grandson on my mother's side, the only grandson on my father's side, along with being born on my grandmother's birthday, I led a charmed life for a few early years.

As I got older, I enjoyed the position with my mother that most sons enjoy: that of being able to do no wrong—that is, until my antics reached the point that even she just couldn't take it anymore. All the while, my dad just shook his head and exhibited a variety of pained facial expressions expressing his annoyance and dismay with whatever my most current activities might have been.

My educational experience was, for the most part, nondescript. In high school, I concentrated more on trying to beat the system than applying the talents that I had been blessed with—a process that found me expelled my senior year over a prank and brawling during a baccalaureate ceremony. I always felt that I was smarter than most of those who stood in front of me to instruct, and with a few exceptions, I'm still not sure that I wasn't right. However, those few exceptions became then, and today are, a part of me.

Higher education wasn't much better. It seemed that my feelings about instructors didn't change much, only I was paying for the pain of listening to people instruct me for whom, again, for the most part, I held utter contempt.

Throughout this entire educational process, I did learn two things: never accept "no" for an answer, and never believe that something couldn't be done ... both of which would serve me well in future endeavors.

Sometime during my pursuit of a higher education, I became interested in becoming a State Trooper. For the first time, I found myself in a position that had training that I believed made sense and that someday I probably would need to know.

This is when I finally grew up, coming to a quick understanding of life and death and the responsibilities that are placed on lawmen to protect and defend those who are incapable of doing so themselves.

I remember the investigator that did my background investigation prior to my appointment to the training academy. He told me that were I to be successful, I would find that I was entering a career that on a daily basis dealt with people at their best and at their worst, in the most tragic and private of moments to befall their lives, and that in that experience, you either had "it" or you didn't. Of course, with me, this was just one more gauntlet, but all too soon, I learned what he meant ... and I must have had "it" for I have been in some form of that process with others for my entire adult working life.

Law enforcement in those days wasn't as lucrative as it has become today, and many left the field for higher-paying careers. I, too, left for that reason, but I went into what I believed to be a related field, that of internal security with a major airline.

My first several years were spent handling the normal internal security issues. As time passed, I became more involved in issues involving personal employee problems as they involved the interests of the company.

In those days, the Civil Rights Act was only about ten years old, and it was the early days of "equal opportunity" and "nondiscrimination" laws that were rewriting the activities in the workplace. Additionally, an airline is a business that historically had employed many women, both on the front line and in management. This provided for many opportunities to try out the new legislations.

The company that employed me had all the normal problems that large companies and airlines experienced, but somewhat differently than others, the chairman and the president were particular about taking the best care of their employees as possible. This meant that on occasion activities were undertaken by the investigators that might have exceeded what would have been done in another company. This meant that there was a fair amount of experience in involvement in employees' individual personal problems when they were serious enough to warrant that kind of activity.

The other area that was of continual concern was the handling of employees whose personal situations might be of future concern to the safety of the company. One such circumstance provided the basis for my future involvement in stalking investigations.

A pilot, a captain at the airline, was accused of sexual misconduct with a female employee while on duty on an overnight. This was an individual who had previous allegations regarding his conduct. I was directed to investigate and determine if there was any substance to the allegation and, if so, attempt to prove the claims that had been made, or to dispel the information as false, should that be the case.

The allegations were found to be true, and much worse than believed to be in the beginning. The investigation and subsequent disciplinary action took over a year to complete. During the course of the investigation, approximately twenty women were identified as victims of the misconduct of the pilot in question. In many of the victims' revelations, it was determined that they had not disclosed the information before, to anyone. When these individuals found themselves facing the facts of how they had been victimized, there was a considerable amount of reopening of old wounds. For this reason, the company retained a psychologist to handle these individuals on a case-by-case basis.

As I was the one who was surfacing the information on these victims, and since there was still an active investigation underway, releases were always prepared, which the victims signed, allowing me to be privy to the information and the circumstances of the treatment. During this time, I had a tremendous amount of experience working with the clinical situation that was a part of the investigation that I was handling.

The circumstances of that investigation would provide enough information for a book in and of itself, but that's another subject. Suffice to say that the investigation was successful.

As a result of my relationship with the psychologist, a long-term relationship commenced in which other cases were referred to his care from issues involving the airline.

When I left the airline and undertook my own operation, I determined that I would be involved in general types of investigations. Initially, I gave no consideration to the handling of stalking cases. Shortly after it was made known that I was starting a business, I was contacted by my old friend, the doctor, and we discussed the feasibility of someone of my background handling referrals from the doctor in cases relating to stalking and abuse. Thus began my involvement in the protection of stalking victims.

There are many individuals that are well qualified to discuss issues of stalking ... and as many as there are, there is an equal number of philosophies on the appropriate methods of handling. On some issues experts disagree, but there are many philosophies that are constants. This book is not a compendium of stalking stories. I will occasionally refer to a situation in which I was involved (with names and cities disguised), but it won't be an effort to tell that story as much as to give an example.

Considering yourself an expert in any field is a bold undertaking, especially when those reading your words may be living in harm's way, looking to someone for guidance. I won't call myself an expert—rather, one who has had immense experience in this area.

Should you be looking for an understanding of what stalking is, this book will do the job. Should you be one of those who believe that they may be being victimized by a stalker, this book will not solve your problem; but hopefully, it will help you identify whether or not there is a problem and, hopefully, give you an understanding of the process necessary to protect yourself.

So, now you know about me. Let's learn about stalking.

Joseph E. Rice

CHAPTER 2
HOW DID WE GET HERE?

Many years ago, when I was just beginning to understand the fascinations of the opposite sex, I can recall a variety of rules of conduct strongly suggested to me by my father … let's call these the "epistles of inter-sexual conduct according to Ed."

In those days, they weren't so drastic. Actually, they were probably the norm. They all consisted of homespun rules of gentlemanly conduct, which any father would expect be granted to his daughter, and accordingly, exercised when his son was interacting with someone else's daughter. These were things like:

"I don't ever want to hear that you picked up a young lady by simply pulling up and blowing the horn for her to come out or that you didn't walk your date to the door upon arriving at her home at the end of a date."

"If you're going to love women, love them all—short, tall, thin, not so thin, young, not so young, good-looking, not so good-looking. Don't be someone who gets a reputation for only being nice to attractive young women."

"Don't act differently with other women when your wife or girlfriend is present, whatever your personality is; be the same, no matter who is around. Treat any woman the way you would expect someone to treat your sister or your mother or your grandmother."

9

I can remember when I wanted my first car and was told emphatically no. It was explained to me that the particular type of vehicle that I could afford would be one that, as he put it, would not be acceptable should some other joker like me drive up in it intending to take my sister out. Again, the theory was that if the particular "bucket of bolts" wasn't acceptable for your sister, then you weren't going to expose anyone else's sister or daughter to the same experience.

These are simple philosophies, but they weren't that unusual for those days. Most of my friends had the same rules drummed into their heads, and most of the young ladies of the day had fathers who expected this particular standard of treatment.

The basics of conducting yourself as a gentleman went without saying … it was expected prior to, during, and especially after a relationship ended. I can recall a particular instance in which I was going out with a young lady who was a senior at our small high school. I was a sophomore at the time, but most of my friends were older and drove, so I was "in play" earlier than some of the others in my class. We had been out a couple of times, in group settings (four or five other couples), but nothing had progressed anywhere near the area of exclusivity.

Recklessly, as I soon learned, never to repeat, I decided to surprise her at a school function that involved the senior class. I thought that I could meet her after the event and we could go out, then I could take her home. When I arrived, just as the event was ending, I observed her coming out on the arm of one of the fellows from her class. She saw me, excused herself, came over to me, and said that she didn't mean to embarrass or upset me, but that she "didn't know" that I intended to see her that evening. I explained that I too

10

was sorry, that it was just a spur of the moment thing, and not to worry, and that it was okay. That was all well and good until I got out of there. I don't recall being so upset to that point in my young and inexperienced life.

When I got home, I was still not happy, and my displeasure was obviously apparent to my family, in particular, my father. He escorted me to the basement and had me explain exactly what had occurred that had upset me so. He listened intently and compassionately, asking a few appropriate questions, and after a considerable evaluation of the incident, he looked me in the eye and simply said, "Grow up! If you're going to date, things won't always go your way, and if you'd been considerate enough to let the young lady know of your plans, neither of you would have been put into the embarrassing situation that you just experienced." And most importantly, he added, "I don't intend to go through this every time something doesn't go your way."

Several years ago, a young man I worked with was married to a young woman who had been married before. She had a five-year-old son to whom my acquaintance had become extremely attached. The marriage lasted less than two years, and shortly after they separated, she applied to become a flight attendant at the airline where he was employed. After she had gone through the interview and screening process, he was contacted by a company officer, with whom he was a close friend, and asked if he wanted her to fail in her attempt to become a flight attendant. He asked how she had done in the screening and was told that she was successful, that the only step left was to notify her to report to training, and that he could stop it if he just said the word. He told his friend that if she was qualified, she should be given the opportunity, and that he had no intention of becoming involved in preventing her from getting the position that she sought.

11

This little story isn't about the young man as much as it's about the times. I don't believe that he gave his decision a second thought. It was no longer his business what she did, and he had no right to interfere in any fashion … to say nothing about the actions of the company officer.

Having said that, we, as a society, seem to have lost most of the chivalry that existed not so many years ago. Some might blame the women's movement, but I don't for a second. I believe that most of the interaction between men and women that occurred a few years ago will still work and be acceptable today when done appropriately and, most importantly, in the right spirit.

Stalking victims can be either male or female, although most are female. Most of the discussions in this book and most of my experiences have involved female victims.

It seems that the "have anything you want" philosophy that has been so pervasive for the last few years has intruded into the relationships between individuals, thus creating the theory that "if I can't have you, then no one else will," or "if you don't want me, I'll destroy you." Now, these are referring to individuals that possess a degree of narcissistic understanding (oversimplified, they're always right).

Individuals who are truly mentally ill tend to defy reason. (You can't reason with a person who has no capacity to reason.)

Those who become stalkers come in many forms, but the core constituents of their personalities tend to be similar, regardless of their station in life. For instance, I have had personal experience with a variety of individuals who were stalkers, and their backgrounds were extremely diverse—a painting contractor, a bank executive, a mountain man who was the victim's handyman, an insurance salesman, a former female student of the female victim, and an unemployed young artist, to name a few. As is apparent, the person's personal situation or career path has nothing to do with whether he or she might choose to be a stalker ... but his or her personal psychological make-up has everything to do with his or her future actions, and additionally, it may determine just how difficult it will be to control and stop his or her activities against the victim.

I have often thought that some of today's problems in this area are the result of the "me" generation—that being that everything is supposed to be the way that "I" want it, and whatever I want, I can have.

We are currently observing this style of "life" in every aspect of society. When those of my generation were young, we had to learn to make decisions on our choices at a very young age. We were told to decide what we wanted to do most or what was most important to us, and that was the activity in which we could become involved. It was made very clear that "you can't do everything."

The variety of activities available today, from daycare forward into the educational process, are overwhelming for parents who haven't learned to draw the line ... to say nothing of the destructiveness that is being wreaked upon the family unit. Young boys and men of today spend every free moment in the pursuit of athletic or other activity excellence with no possible consideration of activities with a father or grandfather.

However, it isn't just the system or the young people. The parents are the major part of the problem, in that they have the ability to say no. But for want of little Johnny missing out on something that the neighbor's son has done, we'll do it all—Saturday morning with basketball practice at 8:00, the soccer game at 11:00, Mary Sue's birthday party at 3:00, and roller skating with the gang at 6:00; church Sunday morning at 9:00, softball tryouts at 1:00, soccer game at 3:00, and movies at 7:00. Just think, in only four years, this twelve-year-old will be able to drive and haul himself around to all these activities, instead of the parents being the chauffeur, coach, and valet, which they have been for ten years, ages six to sixteen.

So, when a young woman tells little Johnny, "No, I don't want to go out with you anymore," it may be the first time in his young, spoiled life that he has ever been told no!

Now, I wouldn't begin to suggest that this is the sole reason for the ills of today, as many who are stalkers are older than this generation. There is a myriad of societal reasons that may be contributors. Functional, mentally ill persons seem to have become apparent most everywhere … and the distance between functional and dis-functional is a short trip. All it may take to drive someone who is barely "hanging on" to his stability is to deny him something or someone to which he believes that he is entitled.

The overwhelming number of domestic crises that exist today, spawning the great number of child custody issues, is certainly a contributor. More and more cases today are appearing in which individuals perceive that their entire lives have been turned upside down, and most of those are incapable of assigning the slightest amount of blame on themselves, causing them to look for the nearest lightning rod to be the recipient of their "bolts of blame."

Enter the woman, who, through her selfish, self-centered inconsideration, is now the cause for all his distress and the utter and total destruction of his life.

If these guys were totally bent on self-destruction, and we could be assured that they would only hurt themselves, as horrible as the loss of any life may be, the entire arena of self-protection for the person to whom they assign the blame would be much simpler. But in all too many documented cases, they don't want to go alone ... and why should they? They've never accepted blame for anything yet.

Then there are the times when the bad guy sets his desires (or sights) on a victim, and there is no understandable reason that is apparent to anyone but him.

It seemed that once upon a time, the wounded suitor possessed some measurable amount of dignity. That dignity, along with a certain amount of embarrassment drove a demeanor of behavior that, while not always pleasant, was far from dangerous. Those days are gone, and to attempt to analyze the ills of society to understand stalking is the stuff of several volumes of books that might still not be able to answer the questions. Suffice to say, the day when a woman could feel comfortable in walking away from a relationship involving a man is a train that has left the station.

Joseph E. Rice

CHAPTER 3
WHO IS A STALKER?

In a simple definition, Mr. Webster defines stalking as "**to pursue or approach ... to prey ... stealthily ....**"

The legal system varies from state to state, but generally speaking, most states have enacted laws regarding an individual's activity "**... intended to prohibit the engaging in a pattern of conduct designed to knowingly cause another to believe that the offender will cause physical harm to the other person.**"

The legal appropriateness of various laws varies with the circumstances of the actual activity in question. For instance, one law may be appropriate if the victim and the stalker are, or were, married; or if they were not married, but romantically involved; or if they only knew each other; or in some circumstances, when they have never met. The degree of involvement or relationship, or lack thereof, between the victim and stalker is extremely critical in determining, first of all, if there are appropriate legal remedies, and just what remedies would be appropriate.

However, the overwhelming problem that occurs in many cases is the fact that little can be done until the activities of a stalker reach the level of law breaking. In the meantime, considerable psychological damage can be done to a victim while the authorities are relatively helpless to assist.

As we discussed in a previous chapter, stalkers come from a variety of personas. Some are prominent citizens, some are thugs, some are average individuals who are wounded suitors who just couldn't handle what may have happened to them, and some may have mental deficiencies, recognizing that any stalker has some degree of mental deficiency.

Most all of us are familiar with the California stalking case involving the actress Rebecca Schaeffer, from the television sitcom *My Sister Sam*, who was stalked by a deranged fan who ultimately killed her. This was the beginning of the movement in California to enact legislation to protect innocent victims from stalkers. That movement spread throughout the nation, giving rise to much of the legislation that we see today.

Celebrity victims are a special group. In many cases, they don't know their stalker. He or she is a stranger who has become enamored with the victim's public persona and has become obsessed. The stalker believes that if only left to his or her own devices, surely the victim would ultimately see the light and want to be with him or her.

Another uniqueness of the celebrity victim is that they usually get immediate attention from the authorities, and any private investigation or security is easily affordable.

Most stalkers are not in the celebrity arena. They are victimizing average people in average lives.

Usually a female victim has had some degree of relationship with her stalker. Husbands who are estranged, former husbands, boyfriends all have one thing in common ... the fact that something happened to them, something was taken from them, so they feel a loss. The loss can be in the form of love, sexual gratification, embarrassment, humiliation, or it can be monetary. The common thread in all their problems is that they perceive the victim, correctly or incorrectly, to be the sole cause of their predicament.

Understand that the victim may have done nothing to warrant the beliefs of the stalker ... or the stalker's theory of the root of his problem may be absolutely correct. This isn't to say that the victim should be precluded from making decisions and taking actions that are believed to be in her best interest, but let us not forget that the stalker is incapable of assigning any degree of blame on himself.

Stalkers can be powerful individuals who aren't used to being denied anything that they want. The origin of the problem may be as simple as a victim wanting to end the relationship, with the stalker relating the victim's rebuff to that of a subordinate refusing to do something that the stalker, the powerful person, had ordered him to do. In the stalker's mind, he is the supervisor and the victim is the subordinate in every way, shape, and form.

Some stalkers are just the average guy who makes the victim's acquaintance, and they choose to begin seeing each other socially. Sometimes the problems begin upon the breakup of a tumultuous relationship, and other times, the relationship has been relatively normal, and the end is thought to be rather peaceful by the victim.

Either simultaneously with the breakup or sometime soon after the relationship has ended, in the mind of the victim, it becomes apparently clear that the stalker has failed to accept the fact that things as he knew them are no more. He is facing the pain of a loss, which is normal; he may be dealing with a degree of embarrassment (depending on the particular circumstances of the situation), which is normal to a degree; and he may be dealing with anger, which too can be normal, to a degree. So, if all these feelings that a stalker may be having can be normal, what makes him different from another individual that leaves a relationship and does not become a stalker?

There are certainly psychological explanations for most all of the activities that anyone performs today, and the stalker is no exception. But we aren't trying to be clinicians here, we're just trying to help you understand in layman's terms the makeup of the stalker.

The difference is that many of the feelings that the stalker has are normal for someone who has experienced an unexpected and unwanted loss, but the average person allows his mind to begin the healing process. He draws on the depth of his experience to begin the healing. He is able to realize that if he really cared for someone at one time, then he would want that person to be happy, and if that means being without him, then, not immediately but eventually, he's okay with that. What a great guy!

Now, I realize that not all normal breakups work out this well, but there is a great distance between the ideal and the stalker. Usually, when we delve into the background of the stalker, we find things such as the lack of a strong male influence in his life, being raised with few rules, consistently having his own way, not having to work for anything, and a general history of some form of dysfunctionality.

Some stalkers come from backgrounds of emotional or sexual abuse that they experienced as a child. They have been raised in an environment in which they were the victims, and now, their own lives are totally consumed by the drive for control and power over others.

Said differently, let's say you knew an extremely selfish and spoiled young boy, who may not have had the best childhood. If you added twenty years or so to his age, leaving his bad habits and personality traits in place, you would have the primary ingredient for a stalker. Now, just because a man is selfish and spoiled doesn't mean that he'll always be a stalker. He may just be selfish and spoiled. However, most stalkers possess some form of these traits accompanied by other, more severe mental thoughts and actions.

The situation which involves the marital breakup and turns into a stalking situation has both positives and negatives. The positive is the fact that the victim should know the personality and the habits of the stalker extremely well ... after all, she has been married to him. The negative is the fact that the marriage has provided for the ability of many more entanglements that are much more difficult to unravel. For instance, children, which create an immediate difficulty in separation and the elimination of contact between the parties. Joint relationships that have existed throughout the time that the stalker and his victim were married can be difficult for the victim to extract herself from should the stalker continue to maintain the relationships. (Suggestions on the handling of these situations will be discussed in later chapters.)

But as in other stalking situations, the root causes are the same: embarrassment and sense of loss. It is just that the method and success of handling a stalking situation is directly proportional to the type and extent of the existing relationship prior to the breakup.

The stalker who is suffering from a mental deficiency is by far the most difficult to deal with for a variety of reasons. First of all, the predictability of the stalker's actions is extremely difficult, and the methods of arresting his behavior that would be successful on stalkers of more stability do not have the same success.

All sizes and shapes, you bet ... but at the root is a baseline that says, I am more powerful than you; I'm more important than you; without me, you're nothing; what you want doesn't matter; you have something that is mine; if I can't have you, no one will; or if you don't give in, I'll destroy you.

Make no mistake, regardless of the type of stalker, these are the reasons. The only difference is the degree to which the stalker takes his actions before coming to his senses, or being stopped by other means.

CHAPTER 4
WHO IS A VICTIM? ARE YOU A VICTIM? HOW DO YOU KNOW?

WE ONLY GET HURT BY THOSE CLOSE TO US!

The mere fact that you are reading this book gives rise to certain questions ... Are you reading this information out of a sense of curiosity, or are you trying to answer questions that may be troubling you in your personal life? If the latter is the case, I suspect that you are currently in or may be in the beginning stages of a problem.

Nearly anyone can become a victim. This isn't an exclusive group, limited only to those of lesser intelligence, those of lesser financial standing, those who are timid and shy, and those who by most standards, their own and those with whom they are acquainted, are not powerful individuals.

Victims of stalkers come from all positions in society. I have represented businesswomen who were vice presidents, wives of wealthy individuals, school teachers, average women who were secretaries, and stay-at-home, unemployed moms during and after their divorces. The victims come in all financial groups: those with great resources and those of not-so-great means. There is no common denominator in the victims … however, as we have said before, there are common denominators in the stalkers.

Becoming a victim isn't something that has a lack of warning signs. When we take a forensic look at the relationship that existed prior to the crisis behavior, there are usually signs that an outsider would have clearly seen. In many cases, the victim herself will admit that she recognized some of the signs and chose to ignore them, but in many cases, those who are close to you have a wide berth when it comes to their behavior and so does the potential stalker.

As I stated in the heading for this chapter, "We only get hurt by those close to us." This isn't as profound a statement as it might seem, but when you analyze it, I know that I have found, and I think that you too will find, it to be true. When considering those who we would consider enemies, we are guarded. They aren't privy to personal information about us, our personal habits, our finances, our work and leisure routines, our friends, and any number of other confidences reserved for those close to us. Not so with our friends … we share it all. It has been said that the benefit of having a close friend or a mate is that you have someone to share things with, good and bad. This is a wonderful process to experience, but when things go bad, and the former mate or friend becomes the enemy, or stalker, he is immediately armed with volumes of information that can be used to disrupt the life of and conceivably harm the victim.

Does this mean that we should never have a close friend, mate, or confidant? Certainly not, but it does mean that if things turn sour, the bad guy has a giant head start. While you're trying to accept the fact that he would even do such things to you, having once been so close, he's already planning his next move. The fact that you were close is the very thing that enables him to have the knowledge to systematically attack the foundations of your stability.

There are exceptions to this, such as the individual who is emotionally unstable and the individual who has only a brief encounter with the victim and becomes enamored. But in most cases, the stalker is operating from an acquired base that was generously provided by a willing, cooperative future victim.

To recognize whether or not you are a victim, it is necessary to understand the degrees of stalking. There are hundreds of subtle, legal ways to begin the systematic unraveling of the victim's life that fall well short of violations of the law. So, the first step in recognizing if you are or may become victimized is to return to our basic makeup of the stalker. He is spoiled and selfish. You have taken something from him that he either wants or perceives that he wants … you. The relationship, such as it might have been, is over in your mind, and he may fail to accept that and accepts no blame for that result.

Now, assuming that you understand that you are perceived to be the cause of loss to the potential stalker, it is time to start paying attention to that which you formerly did not.

Little things that previously only seemed strange now bear paying attention to such as disruptions in your daily routine that you did not cause, disruptions in the operation of your residence (utilities, maintenance help, etc.), disruptions in your finances, or damage to or maintenance problems with your vehicles. These are the beginnings of "testing the water," so to speak, in a stalking process that may escalate to more serious actions.

Protecting yourself doesn't have to require paranoia, but merely an intensified level of awareness. You have had a close friend, a partner, a confidant that has now become a potential adversary. You must change your philosophy. Till you know differently, you should assume that this wounded person may choose to repair his ruffled feathers by trying to disrupt yours, either to show you the pain that he is feeling or, in some twisted way, to "beat" you into submission so that you will come running back to him.

The differences in experiences with former associates after breakups will obviously vary from case to case. For instance, your person may have never taken an interest in personal issues involving your activities. If that suddenly occurs, either through contact with you or being related to you by other friends, take notice. However, if your person always paid close attention to your activities, it may be that it is just taking awhile for the realities to settle in that it is no longer his business. If your person was never attentive to issues involving things such as your car or the house, but suddenly takes an interest in those things, take note. If your person previously had no interest in your employment, but suddenly takes an interest in your job, again, take note. Sometimes these are the subtle beginnings of information gathering that may set the stage for future problems. Often they are cloaked in the robes of concern: "I have never paid attention to your needs and problems, and I want to make it up to you." Remember, if you're still together, these may be initial signs of things to come. If you're no longer together, the contact needs to be eliminated … if not, you are providing an "information highway" that may be a shortcut to disaster.

Idle conversation such as, "How's it going?" "Where were you last night?" "Who were you with?" etc. are all "fishing trips" that can provide the "bait" for a future encounter that may not be pleasant.

Just remember, the biggest source of information about you is you. Your words, your body language, and your actions that your former comrade had learned to read are all the "intelligence" that he needs to make plans intent on disrupting your life. The smaller his storehouse of knowledge, the harder it is to affect your life.

But as we have said before, the probability that you may be a future or current victim is most easily recognized in the subtle changes that may be occurring in his personality, and the expert at recognizing those changes is you. It's tough enough to deal with these situations in the best of circumstances; you don't need to help your adversary.

Joseph E. Rice

CHAPTER 5
HOW DO YOU BEGIN TO PROTECT YOURSELF?

ALL ABOUT YOU

When considering a stalking environment, if you conjure up any possible scenario having you as the victim that doesn't place you, your safety, or your ability to safely live your daily life without interruption in jeopardy—any compilation of processes in which the primary focus is not you—you just don't get it. This is all about you, your habits, your desires, your safety, your ability to exist in freedom from harm and freedom from fear.

What is not of concern is how Johnnie's soccer or baseball schedule conflicts with your situation, or the bad guy's host of problems that is causing his menacing behavior, or your former mutual friends and their perception of the situation, or anything else that may cross your mind … other than you and either what it takes to make this go away or what it takes to get it under some degree of control. What you have to understand is this: If you take care of yourself first, all the rest of the issues that you may have considered will take care of themselves.

If you've been on a commercial airline, I'm sure you recall the announcement that the flight attendants make when they're telling you how to use the oxygen masks. "If you are traveling with a small child or anyone else that may need assistance, put on your mask first, then assist the other person." Why? If you pass out from lack of oxygen and topple over, you're not going to be much help to anyone else. Stalking victims are in the same proverbial boat. You have to develop a philosophy of helping yourself first, then concentrate on the rest of the world for which you feel that you may have some degree of responsibility.

As we have discussed, stalking victims come in all shapes and sizes, from all walks of life and in all stations of society. A victim is often one who has been victimized before in other situations. For instance, it is not unusual for a victim to have had problems with previous male associates, either at work or in her personal relationships. It is easy for someone not involved in the problem who may never have had a similar problem to point out that this is not the first time that the victim has had a bad experience that resulted from a relationship with a man. Usually this brings forth the exclamation, "Is this a habit with her?"

Well, to a point, yes, it could be. Personalities of people are the primary ingredients in their success or lack thereof in interactions with others. In other words, how do they get along, are they well liked, are others content to be in their company? This can apply to interactions in the workplace and in personal relationships. Many times, when speaking of a victim's plight, someone may say, "It's a shame that she is going through that; she's such a nice person." The fact that "she's such a nice person" may have contributed to her being willing to be tolerant of others' faults, lending herself to being taken advantage of and, given all the right components, making herself easy prey for a wounded suitor who chooses to remain instead of go when he is "shown the door."

Individuals such as this lend themselves to repeat incidents, in that their personality does not change. What allowed them to drop their guard and get into trouble before is still part of their personality and will allow it to continue happening, unless it is changed.

This isn't to say that every victim is vulnerable because of her personality. Some victims are extremely strong individuals. There may just be a series of life's incidents that allow them to drop their guard long enough to get into trouble.

When a stalking situation begins as the result of the end of a romantic relationship, it is even more understandable that the victim has allowed herself to be in a vulnerable posture. I often point out to my clients that "we seldom get hurt by our enemies." The reason for this is simple: If someone is considered to be an enemy of yours, you probably don't allow him to become privy to an entire host of personal information concerning you, thus not arming him with a volume of information that can be used to turn your life upside down. However, when it is someone you once trusted, this type of stalking situation necessitates that the victim become even more creative in her efforts to mask her habits and routines from the stalker. Remember, you probably didn't get into this situation overnight, and most probably, you weren't too cautious with information concerning yourself … so the remedy isn't going to be overnight, and overcoming all the information that you have already provided to the bad guy will also take awhile and be quite a job.

In the case of the stalker who is acting through a mental deficiency, the victim may have done absolutely nothing. With this type of bad guy, there is no discernable reason; it is a matter of perception on his part. Whatever he thinks to be the facts of the situation is the case, for he can only visualize things in his own mind.

"IF YOU DON'T THINK YOU'RE JOHN WAYNE, NO ONE ELSE WILL." —John Kopp, Coach

As we just said, being stalked is a personal thing—extremely personal—and efforts that may be employed to eliminate or mitigate the actions of the stalker are also of the most personal nature.

Most victims haven't lived their lives in some variation of harm's way, so all this is a crisis that has never been experienced before. They find that they have lived relatively normal, sometimes even quiet, lives, and suddenly, they are literally fighting for their safety, sanity, and sometimes their lives.

To paraphrase our subtitle, if you don't think that you can beat this, then you're already beaten. Granted, sometimes it takes support and encouragement, but the most important part of the plan is your conviction in not being beaten.

This isn't to suggest that it will be easy or that you won't have to make great changes in your daily habits. You may have to make some new friends and part company with some old ones who knew you both. But if you're committed to beating this guy, if you're committed to taking your life back, if you're committed to showing this guy that he doesn't own you and that he can't destroy you, if you're ready "to throw him under the bus" (figuratively) to regain your persona as you once knew it, you can succeed.

The problem occurs when a victim fails to act. You may perceive your inactivity as a sign of compassion or consideration, while the stalker perceives that same lack of action as weakness and/or fear, usually causing him to escalate his activity, thinking that it is working and that he is winning. Sometimes the first actions of defense can be as simple as letting him know that he isn't dealing with the same old girl. Alice doesn't live here anymore, but the lady that does is mad as hell and isn't going to take it anymore!

One of the examples that I like to use in explaining to victims how they have to demonstrate that they are capable of taking care of themselves goes something like this:

While I don't know what part of the country in which you reside, it's safe to say that you have some familiarity with the highway patrol or state police in your area. (Now, let me make this clear from the start, this isn't a comparison of various law enforcement agencies, it is merely an example … one in which any law enforcement agency could be interjected.)

So, back to our state police story. If you've never taken time to observe any of these individuals, do so the next time you see some poor unfortunate "schmuck" getting a speeding ticket. Notice the size of the trooper; is he a giant? Is it even a he? It is fair to say that as a state trooper goes through his or her career, most probably he or she will have occasion to arrest or certainly encounter someone who, in the situation in which he or she finds his or her self, is not happy. Do you think that your state troopers will be bigger, tougher, and stronger than everyone they encounter? Will they be a better fighter than everyone they encounter? Take the word of one whose personal experience can tell you, the answer is a resounding NO!

So, how is it that a state trooper who may be of lesser size and ability and who deals with a hostile public on a daily basis, is usually successful in whatever he is trying to accomplish and seldom gets hurt? State troopers aren't allowed to shoot everyone that gives them a rough time—although I have to confess, it does cross their minds more than most people would care to believe.

So, what magic allows them to be successful? Could it be respect? Could it be the fear of the unknown? Those they encounter, even if they don't respect the law or the trooper, just don't know what that trooper is capable of, even if it is a female trooper or a male trooper of lesser size.

The adversary of the trooper knows that troopers are trained, that they have certain tools available to them, that they can call for help, and that the consequences of challenging them, or worse, can have devastating results. Guess what; you can have all these qualities in defending yourself.

Let's talk about one more thing that our trooper has going for him. Our trooper is expecting the worst from the bad guy and is ready to deal with it. There's no feeling sorry for him, there's no sympathy for him, and there's no consideration for what he once was. There's only one thought process: This guy's a bad guy that might try to hurt me, and that's not going to happen. You can apply this same thought process to your bad guy.

So, are you bigger, stronger, a better fighter, able to leap tall buildings with a single bound? Probably not. But can you defend yourself; you bet you can!

Let's touch on one other form of female defense. As I told you in the beginning of this book, I'm not a psychologist or psychiatrist, but I've had a fair amount of experience in the areas of which I speak. Not to be sexist, but men are mental wimps. (That should totally annoy the rest of my gender.) What I mean is that when it comes to physical strength, the men usually win, but when the game calls for mental strength, it goes to the gals, hands down.

I have experienced women in the worst of situations, and once they crossed that mental bridge that showed them the way to resolution in their mind and found that they could handle the situation, everyone else had better be on the same road heading to the same destination, for there is no deterring them from their destination. Simply said, in my experience, women in crisis are immensely more mentally tough than their male counterparts.

So, what have we got here? You can learn everything that you need to know to protect yourself, you can put together the appropriate tools to do so, and you are blessed with a God-given ability to be mentally tougher than your adversary.

You can do this … if you think you're John Wayne. And if you do, most everyone else will too, and those that aren't sure will be afraid to ask.

DOCTOR, WHENEVER I RAISE MY ARM LIKE THIS, IT HURTS. WHAT SHOULD I DO?

I'm sure we've all heard the story of the patient that tells his doctor that whenever he raises his arm in a certain position, it hurts, and then asks what he should do. The doctor's reply is, of course, "Then don't raise your arm that way."

If someone believes that she can begin to get through a stalking or harassment situation without great changes in her personal life, she simply doesn't know what she's talking about. She may feel that her personal activities are being restrained, her freedom is being restricted, and her personal rights are being violated. If she does, she's right.

One of the first defenses to any type of situation in which the safety of an individual is of concern is called "avoiding the threat." Now, obviously this isn't possible in every situation that you may encounter, but in the activities and habits of your daily life that are predictable and routine, you can make efforts to avoid the threat.

I can recall a particular case in which the victim was concerned that the stalker was always in contact with mutual friends and acquaintances. He was always discussing their particular situation, which armed them with his version of facts, which caused them to feel the need to attempt to talk with her about the subject. It seemed that each time the victim went to the local health club to work out, she would encounter someone who wanted to talk. Not only did she not care to discuss things with anyone else, this was also creating an indirect line of communication with the stalker.

The obvious question was how to stop this, with an even more obvious solution … stop going to that health club, which she did.

If you have seen a professional fighter enter the arena to make his walk to the ring or a rock star traveling through a crowd, it's not hard to spot their security. They're the ones surrounding the celebrity; they're the ones that look like thugs, adorned in tight-fitting T-shirts and pounds and pounds of gold jewelry. They usually travel through the largest crowd along the most direct route, daring anyone to come near.

The converse situation is the politician or the CEO. Were you to encounter either of these individuals on the street, and you happened to recognize him or her, you would be hard-pressed to discern who among the group the security was. I do however realize that we can all recognize the President's Secret Service. They're the ones with the little speakers in their ears, and they talk to their wrists.

Should the security surrounding a member of the professions that I have just described happen to perceive something that they believe to be a threat to their charge, and should you happen to be in the proximity of this situation, you would run a serious risk of harm during their defensive posture. Might this come from stray gunfire? Most probably not. Rather, you might get trampled as they spirited their responsibility away from the threat.

"But, they have guns," you say. "Automatic pistols, Uzis," you say. "And they're all trained professionals," you say. And you would be correct. "But why wouldn't they fight?" you ask, and I would tell you that you already answered that question. They're trained professionals, exercising the first, most important rule of defense: Get out of harm's way. There is no good reason for anyone to enter into a competition that has even the minute chance of defeat when you can get out of there and increase your odds of defeat to zero.

More importantly, you can eliminate any amount of risk by avoiding the possible incident completely, by not being there in the first place. Intentionally or knowingly entering into harm's way is for those brave souls in our armed forces, law enforcement, and John Wayne, who you are not; remember, we just think that you are.

To return to our example, if the security surrounding our politician or CEO were doing their advance work in the days previous to the incident that we used for our example, and in the course of that preparation were to determine that area or that situation to be a potential threat risk to the person of their responsibility, most assuredly the schedule would be changed to avoid that area and that potential confrontation completely. That isn't to say that occasionally this rule isn't bent for some extremely important reason, but for the most part, "executive protection details" protect best by solid "threat assessment" and avoiding the threat.

As you have now found yourself in a situation that can conceivably place you in harm's way at any given time, you have to begin applying a threat assessment to the planning of your daily activities. You need to determine the potential risk of a confrontation with your bad guy in any location that you intend to find yourself.

"HAVE YOU EVER DANCED WITH THE DEVIL IN THE PALE MOONLIGHT?" —The "Joker," *Batman*

A female business executive in a Midwestern city had been seeing a man that she had met in the course of her business affairs. He, too, was an extremely successful executive in the same city, although he lived in another state. His weekly routine was to spend three to four days a week in the city in which his company was located and then return to his home for the weekend, sometimes working several days from a home office. Weekends had been sparse for the two of them, since he was usually out of town. The story was that he had been married many years ago and had grown children. After a few missed holidays and his continual absence on the weekends, her curiosity got the best of her. When she

38

challenged him as to her concerns, a series of attempts were made to convince her that he was indeed divorced, when in actuality, he was married with a family in the city in which he resided.

Upon learning of his true situation, she immediately terminated the relationship. This was not to his liking, but he feigned acceptance for her benefit. He did continue to call, attempting to be helpful and concerned about her daily life.

When he began to invade certain private information, which caused her to believe that he had some method of electronic eavesdropping in place, and when he began questioning her about her activities during a recent vacation, suggesting possible pictures and contact with someone from another state who had been involved in her vacation, she retained me to have an electronic sweep done at her home.

In discussing her situation, it became apparent that she had been having phone contacts with the individual and that she had even accompanied him to assist him in a purchase in which he believed that she could be of assistance. I asked her if the relationship was over, and she said that it was. I pointed out to her that she hadn't made that clear to him and that she was "dancing with the devil."

She was allowing a line of communication to exist that was keeping him "in the ballgame," and no matter how veiled she made her conversations with him, she was still inadvertently transmitting necessary information to him that allowed him to manipulate her.

One classic example of this theory is well known in the law enforcement community involving hostage situations.

Any hostage negotiator will tell you that the most important thing that needs to happen in a hostage negotiation is to establish contact with the hostage taker and keep that line of communication open. Why? While there is communication, there is a chance to convince him to change his mind and alter the course of his behavior. In that situation, communication is a good thing … in a potential stalking situation, it's a bad thing.

In another case in which I was associated, the victim had been involved in a long-term relationship with the stalker. Prior to my entering the case, she had tried a variety of methods to convince him that it was "time to go." Her situation had been exacerbated by the fact that she traveled in her job approximately fifty percent of the time. While this made the situation easier to tolerate, it created an environment which made bringing it to a conclusion much more difficult.

During this period of attempting to extricate herself from the situation, her bad guy got into trouble with the law. He was charged with a felony and incarcerated. She was notified that for $30,000, a sum that would make restitution and pay the legal fees, he could be released and the charges dropped. She agreed to undertake the costs, providing that this would be it; he would get out of her house, get out of her life, and leave her alone. He agreed, only long enough to get out of jail and get the charges dropped. She was "dancing with the devil."

Reading the last few paragraphs, it is easy to second-guess, saying that they should have known better, but it isn't that simple. Remember, success in defending yourself in situations such as this usually requires a complete reversal of your previous posture with the individual in question. Your adversary was a friend, or a lover, and probably a confidant

DON'T LET THE BASTARDS BEAT YOU!

… all persons in which you have had immense trust. Further complicating the issue is the fact that the victims in these cases aren't trained protection professionals. Many times it takes a variety of failed attempts at dealing with the bad guy to convince them of the seriousness of the situation. And so, judging any victim's actions in attempting to deal with a situation in which she has never been is truly counterproductive. After all, this book wasn't available to them back then.

However, taking what we do know about individuals—their personalities, their habits, etc.—and attempting to eliminate emotions before choosing a course of action can greatly increase the level of success in your actions. I know that saying you should eliminate emotions from your decision-making process is much easier said than done. In these cases, those emotions run the gamut from anger, frustration, love, compassion, fear, and depending on the time the situation has gone on, sometimes hate.

But there is a simple method of analysis that can be applied to any potential action. It goes something like this: If you are trying to get out or trying to get him out, and he's ignoring your wishes, what would cause you to believe that he would respect any possible "deal" that you attempt to make with him to leave you alone?

Remember this: You're in this situation because he is a bad guy. Being a bad guy isn't a momentary event; it's probably a way of life that you may not have recognized with him before you became the recipient of his bad acts.

IF YOU HAVE TO THINK ABOUT WHETHER IT'S RIGHT OR WRONG … IT'S PROBABLY WRONG

41

I first became familiar with this old truth many years ago in dealing with my father. When being questioned about my most recent excursion of aberrant behavior, I would attempt my defense by beginning with, "I thought that—" I would usually be cut off with his version of the phrase, "Don't you realize that if you have to think about whether it's right or wrong, it's probably wrong?"

Over the years, it has been eerie how many times that homespun logic has been applicable to situations in which I have found myself. It is true that many times when something is the appropriate act for the situation at hand, the answer is forthcoming and immediate, while in other situations, a contemplated course of action that lends itself to serious thought over the range of possible consequences may be the wrong way to go. It is amazing how taking a moment and applying this logic to the same situation when the answer seems evasive will crystallize immediately the fact that your idea is wrong.

In defending yourself, there will be many occasions in which it is abundantly clear that you can no longer do something as you once did. You're under attack, and you must take a defensive posture. In many cases, this means not going to the same places, not attending functions with the same people, not traveling the same route that you formerly did, and in general, creating a new routine that should involve as much of a lack of routine as possible.

But occasions will occur in which you find yourself giving it more thought than you once would have. These are the occasions in which you should always apply the theory of thinking about whether it's the right choice for you in your present state of affairs.

Remember, the first line of defense is you. We know that your rights are being trampled upon like Sherman marching through Georgia, but that's just how it is, and until things get better, you are the one that has the most control over whether or not you find yourself in harm's way.

SO, LET'S REVIEW THE RULES:

IF YOU DON'T THINK YOU'RE JOHN WAYNE, NO ONE ELSE WILL!

> You must believe that you can beat this situation. If you do, you can succeed. It may take some help, but you can do it. It begins with a state of mind, and no one but you can control your mind. When you are convinced that you're John Wayne, everybody else will believe you!

DOCTOR, WHEN I RAISE MY ARM LIKE THIS, IT HURTS. WHAT SHOULD I DO?

> Your life as you know it is under attack. You can't continue to do the same things at the same places, sometimes with the same people. If what you are about to do may embroil you in a crisis, or hurt you … don't do it!

HAVE YOU EVER DANCED WITH THE DEVIL IN THE PALE MOONLIGHT?

> Bad guys do bad things; you're learning that. You can't bargain with a bad guy and expect a good thing to happen, so don't do it! Don't dance with the devil! ·

IF YOU HAVE TO THINK ABOUT WHETHER IT'S RIGHT OR WRONG, IT'S PROBABLY WRONG!

> Only you can be ultimately responsible for your self-defense. So, when considering actions that you intend to take, ask yourself if it puts you in harm's way, and if the answer isn't an immediate and resounding NO, don't do it; it's probably wrong.

I've used these phrases for a reason. Sometimes in the confusion of the moment, remembering sentences and paragraphs from a book can be difficult. Hopefully, a simple phrase may help you to recall things that we have discussed.

Get these thoughts etched in your head. You'll find them to come in handy ... not only in your protection but also in many of life's little turmoils.

CHAPTER 6
WHAT KIND OF TEAM DO YOU NEED?

"I am the master of my fate; I am the captain of my soul."
—from "Invictus" by William Ernest Henley

We have discussed several times in this book the importance of YOU in the experience of being stalked. Let's go over it again … You are the general, the director of your security, the commander in chief, the "captain of your soul." However you choose to describe your role in this excursion, at some moment it will all be reduced to you and your perception of your ability to overcome this horrible challenge to your very existence.

It has been said that having good taste is easy if you have enough money, and putting together a team to protect you and deal with a serious stalking situation sort of follows the same logic. If you have enough money, it's much easier, and for high-profile victims, this is usually the case. Unfortunately, most victims of these types of incidents are not wealthy, and when resources are sparse, innovation has to be plentiful.

So, let us begin by reviewing those areas that we have already discussed.

Family and Friends

> It is absolutely essential, during the time when your life is under the stress created by this type of

situation, that you have some place of peace and safety. This can be provided by family or close friends; however, they must clearly be on your team, even though they may believe that you may be incorrect in some of your judgments. Any friend or family member must be—let us repeat that, MUST BE—with you, or he or she is against you. Simple logic, dramatic logic, but oh-so-true logic. There cannot be anyone "in your camp" who is a sympathizer with the other side.

Assuming that they meet the criteria, having family and friends in a location to go to and be safe, or living in a location in which family and friends are readily available for support, is tremendously beneficial to keeping you not only safe, but also stable.

Psychological Counselor

As should be apparent to you by now, to successfully guide yourself through the muddy waters that we have been discussing requires a "steady hand at the helm." Said differently, you can't get through the complexities of keeping yourself safe while still living the rest of your life as normally as possible if you have become psychologically unstable.

The assistance of an appropriate counselor can be invaluable for a variety of reasons; however, from the standpoint of dealing with the immediate crisis of you being victimized by a stalker, there are primarily two major areas in which a psychologist can be most beneficial.

The first and most obvious is experiencing the process of counseling and receiving help to emotionally stabilize you during a time in which you are being exposed to experiences, the likes of which you have probably never conceived and certainly never experienced.

The second area of primary assistance to you and to anyone dealing with your problem is that of listening to your experiences and helping you sort through the differences between that which is a real activity against you and that which is a product of a panicked inability to reason. Recognizing incidents and actions against you that you may not have previously identified as problems, may expose psychological habits and traits of your adversary that need to be brought to the attention of those who are assisting you with your problem.

Certainly there are many other benefits to counseling, not the least of which is helping to put this all behind you—as best as can be done—and assisting you with moving on with your life. However, the areas that I have suggested are those that are most critical to the immediate situation in which you now find yourself.

Protection/Security Professional

The retention of an individual that specializes in the protection of individuals from harm by others can be extremely valuable to you if you have the appropriate resources.

The benefits of such an arrangement come from several areas of activity. The most obvious being that of working closely with you to insure that you are taking the appropriate steps to protect yourself. As we have discussed, sometimes the most effective methods of protection are derived from concentrated efforts of avoidance with your adversary ... issues that are sometimes so obvious and simple that, in your trauma, they are elusive. Professional help usually recognizes the obvious.

Those who specialize in the protection of others have extensive experience dealing with the authorities. Working with you to determine the extent of various threats and actions against you, and then conveying those incidents and information to the authorities in a method consistent with that of professional law enforcement procedures creates an air of efficiency that is usually beneficial.

A professional investigator who is engaged by you can provide extensive information to the authorities. This can be of tremendous assistance to your case while the authorities either have not yet taken an interest or the level of activity that you are experiencing has yet to "cross the bar" of that which is illegal.

Your initiative in hiring your own investigator can be an indicator to the authorities of your commitment to professionally dealing with your crisis ... and a demonstration that you are not sitting back leaving the administration of your crisis to others.

Legal Counsel

Retaining an attorney to represent your interests creates an advocate to oversee any of the legal issues that may need guidance through the court system. While protection orders have been streamlined to simplify the process of their issuance, using legal counsel to affect the process, while recognizing that the order that will be issued is the same with or without counsel, involves an officer of the court in the oversight of your problem.

As previously discussed, the legal community is just that, a community of those who are charged with the administration of justice in a particular jurisdiction. When one of their brothers or sisters is representing someone who is in serious trauma, once again, the fact that you have retained professional representation shrouds your problem with a degree of seriousness and commitment that is a positive factor in any dealings that may occur through the law enforcement and legal system.

Additionally, should civil court action be considered as a possible remedy in the resolution of your case, your own attorney is an absolute necessity, and having an attorney who has been involved with you from the inception of your problem is extremely beneficial.

Law Enforcement

From the time that you recognize that you are being victimized, the possibility exists that a law enforcement solution may be the ultimate resolution to your problem. Development of the proper liaison between you, those representing you, and the authorities is imperative to an effective outcome of your crisis. In some cases, victims are successful in developing the appropriate relationship with the authorities on their own, but the process usually unfolds more smoothly with professional help.

Once again, the fact that you have chosen to invest your own time and resources in your problem, rather than simply reporting the situation and leaving it to others, adds a level of commitment and seriousness to their understanding of the problem. Additionally, professional help is more adept at "speaking their language" and, accordingly, assisting the authorities from a professional standpoint and ultimately furthering the execution of the necessary actions to resolve your problem.

In a perfect world, a victim could resolve these problems without having to enlist the assistance of expensive professional help ... of course, in a perfect world, these problems wouldn't have occurred in the first place.

In some cases, the victim is able to wade though the system without help, and obviously, all this help is the ideal situation, but depending on the extent of the problem, varying degrees of assistance can still be helpful if resources are prohibitive.

This is when innovation must overcome resources. Combining your own personal resolve with appropriate professional assistance for the appropriate situations at the appropriate times can greatly lessen the resources necessary to accomplish successful results.

CHAPTER 7
PROTECTION ORDERS
AREN'T BULLETPROOF

Reasonable and prudent actions would not dictate that you approach a rattlesnake sunning himself at the other side of your backyard and poke him with a stick. However, when the animal control people arrive, it surely expedites things if they know that what you observed was indeed a rattlesnake.

I had occasion to work with an attorney in a large Midwestern city who is considered to be the dean of domestic practice in that region. When discussing a particular client's situation, he made the statement that "you do know that protection orders aren't bulletproof." He went on to explain that in his years of practice he had experienced two occasions in which clients of his had obtained protection orders earlier in the day and were that evening homicide victims at the hand of the party toward whom the protection order was directed.

There are several schools of thought about not only the value, but also the judgment of obtaining a protection order. My experience is that it varies greatly from case to case, depending on the circumstances. For instance, some situations may only be exacerbated by the stalker being served with court papers ordering him to appear in court to defend himself against an application for a protection order, and in some other cases, it may be a useful tool in getting the stalker's attention … letting him know that the victim is serious and intends to use the full letter of the law to stop him and protect herself.

The negatives are fairly simple. A protection order puts the stalker before the court as previously stated. Protection orders vary from state to state, and accordingly, their seriousness to the defendant, or the stalker, also varies. In a state such as Florida, a protection order in a domestic case is a criminal charge, as opposed to a civil action. That is, if the victim is successful in obtaining a protection order for domestic violence in Florida, the stalker then has a criminal record. This can have far-reaching ramifications, not only for the stalker, but possibly for the victim. The criminal record can not only inhibit future employment, but in many cases can also create the loss of the stalker's job, which can affect things such as child support and other obligations that the stalker might be providing.

Many states also make a distinction between the type of protection order available to a victim based on the relationship between the victim and the stalker. (Were they married, or were they only acquaintances?)

Probably the largest concern with protection orders is the possibility that a situation that is at the time annoying, albeit illegal, can be caused to escalate to a more seriously dangerous level by throwing the stalker before the courts. This is a valid concern, and those who suggest protection orders at the slightest hint of harassment are treading on a slippery slope.

Once again, the background of the situation, the activities thus far, and the personality of the stalker are all components of the decision-making process. For instance, in the victim's history, has the stalker always been possessive, selfish, and annoying with no hint of violence, or has he been violent? Is he struggling with psychological pressures? Are there other issues that might allow the protection order to push him over the edge, rather than do as it was designed to do, restrain and inhibit his improper behavior?

On the positive side, anytime the authorities are requested to intercede in a "domestic" type of incident, there is always reluctance. This is natural and, to a point, appropriate, in that personal battles between individuals can and do tend to get extremely complicated.

There is always the question of who is at fault, who started the current problem, who has the right to be wherever they are at the time, and will the complainant (the victim) continue to support the action of the authorities should legal action be taken. For these reasons, many states have enacted specific legislation that applies in domestic violence incidents which allows the authorities to make a determination on the appropriate legal action without the consent of the victim, and accordingly, the inability of the victim to withdraw her complaint.

But stalking cases may be less clear than domestic incidents, if that is possible. Upon arrival, the authorities have to decide who is most credible for them to establish a course of action to diffuse and, if appropriate, prosecute the situation.

This is one of the situations in which a protection order is extremely helpful. It is a court order directing that certain actions by the stalker are prohibited. It is usually very clear as to the prohibited circumstances, and it is signed by a judge. This is tremendously helpful to any police officer arriving on the scene. It clearly defines who the players are and what actions are not allowed. Additionally, if the order is found to have been violated, an arrest of the stalker, on the spot, is not only legal, but appropriate.

Another area in which a protection order is helpful is in the response to a victim's complaint. When an order is issued, the local authorities should be notified and given a copy of the order. Should the victim need to notify the police that the stalker is committing some act prohibited by the order (near her house, following her, any activity that has been brought before the judge and made part of the order), it is usually as simple as calling the local authorities, identifying herself, and stating that there is a protection order and that the stalker is in violation of that order.

The alternative to this is calling the police, getting a different dispatcher than the last one with whom you talked and after explaining the entire history of the problem, waiting for the shift supervisor to determine if it is appropriate to have a car respond—all of which is annoying and, more importantly, time consuming.

To suggest that obtaining a protection order should never occur would be as improper as suggesting that in every situation, the first thing that should occur is the filing for an order of protection. Individual cases dictate specific actions. A protection order is simply a tool that can be helpful, when appropriate, in impeding the behavior of the stalker.

CHAPTER 8
VICTIMS AND GUNS
"ANNIE, GET YOUR GUN ... BUT BEST BE READY TO USE IT!"

The subject of firearms and their place in the realm of self-defense is the stuff of entire books, but for our purposes, we shall forgo the philosophical discussions of the subject.

This issue is very simple and basic: to arm or not to arm?

It is incontrovertible that a mother will perform superhuman feats in an effort to protect her children from harm, and while some of the issues that we've been discussing could possibly involve children, most issues involving stalking are not related to the children. This leaves us with the situation involving a woman being called upon to defend primarily herself. When dealing with firearms, this creates an entirely different level of mental performance of the victim.

If there is one overwhelming truth to keep in mind when considering firearms it is this: Consider always the possibility that through mishandling or the inability to use, introducing a firearm into a situation which previously did not have one can have catastrophic results. In street language, if you're not capable of using it, don't bring it to the party; it might get shoved up a part of your anatomy that would be unpleasant, or worse, it could be used on you instead of your adversary.

A firearm and the possession thereof is a complicated issue long before it comes down to being able to effectively use one in the appropriate manner in the appropriate situation. It is always suggested as an easy fix: "You'd better get a gun; you need some protection. If he shows up, you ought to be in a position to blow him away." Great philosophies, but before we get there, let's do some background on the subject.

First of all, there are federal laws that must be complied with, laws that govern the purchase of a firearm (absence of a criminal record, non-addiction to alcohol or drugs, no mental health issues, etc.). Then, most every state has its own set of laws regarding ownership, and depending on what city you live in, they may have another set of local laws. For the most part, we're talking about weapons of self-defense, which means a handgun, which means the most stringent of regulations.

Now, assuming that you can comply with all the laws to own the firearm, you now have to deal with the ability to carry the weapon with you. If this is to be considered a primary method of protecting you, we can't assume that you will only need it when you are in your bedroom and it is in the nightstand beside your bed. If you're accosted by the stalker in the parking lot at the mall, you can't say, "Wait here while I run back to my bedroom and get my gun." It's only of value if it is with you.

The ability to carry a weapon varies from state to state, unless you're in New York where they have the Sullivan Law, and for that, you need to get local guidance. Actually, any weapon ownership and carrying guidance requires local information. Due to many of the Liberal attacks on the second amendment and gun ownership in general, there are constantly changing laws in the states.

Assuming that you do meet the requirements for ownership, concealment and carrying on your person, let's examine some of the restrictions that you will still have to deal with when legally "permitted" under your state's laws.

These are fairly general restrictions from state to state. We don't need to talk about airports and commercial air transportation, do we? If so, understand this, show up at the checkpoint with a gun, and you don't need to be a terrorist to go to jail. Most states restrict carrying a firearm anywhere that serves alcohol, not just the redneck saloon on Dogleg Road, but also the lounge at the Ritz Carlton. They also restrict carrying a firearm in courthouses, schools, hospitals, and anywhere that currently has security and uses metal detectors. Think about why they have the metal detectors, that's your clue.

So, we've complied with ownership laws at every level, and we know where we can carry and where we can't; now all we have to do is get a little training (that we'll talk about shortly) and start carrying. Shall we examine what it means to carry a gun?

Career law enforcement officers, who live with their side arms as much a part of their daily paraphernalia as their pens, can tell anyone what a grandiose pain in the butt it is, and with them, it's a part of their job, not something new and different. You must always know where the weapon is, either on your person or wherever else it may be for a period of time. That someplace must be of the utmost safekeeping, not just under the seat of the car or in a drawer. It must be secure, but still available to the user, hoping that the user isn't the bad guy.

What might this mean to a victim? This isn't meant to be sexist in any way, because the same problems apply to men that are new to the possession of a firearm, but we're talking here about primarily female victims that may now possess a firearm. When was the last time you wanted something that was in your purse, and you couldn't recall where you had placed your purse? When was the last time that you were bringing in items from the car and left something in the car that you intended to bring in? When was the last time that you thought something that you had placed in a certain spot was not where you remembered when you attempted to retrieve it?

These are issues that pertain to keeping the weapon where it is safe and readily accessible. If there happen to be children or anyone else in your home who can't be counted upon to harness their curiosity, the circumstances take on an enhanced responsibility.

Children aren't the only ones who have a natural curiosity about weapons. Many times adults will find a fascination with a gun, and in some ways, they're worse than a child. An intelligent child may realize that it's something that he shouldn't touch, while an adult who is curious has no fear; of course, he also has no sense, but after all, he's an adult.

Understand this: Painful as it may be to the anti-gun crowd, as they say, an unloaded gun never killed anybody. How true, but an unloaded gun does you absolutely no good. If you choose to do this, it has to be loaded and ready at all times. I'm not suggesting that a weapon shouldn't become part of the defense system for a victim, only that it is immensely more complicated than just "getting a gun."

But now that we've decided that we can comply with the appropriate laws, and we've decided that we can conform with the many other impediments to carrying a gun, and we believe that we can remember where it is at all times and keep it safe but accessible, we proceed to purchase a gun.

Usually in purchasing a gun, the salespeople will guide you in your selection once they realize what the intended use is to be. The biggest concern in the selection is that of size and strength to be appropriate for self-defense. For example, an elephant can be brought down with a .308 caliber rifle (30 caliber). What no one says is that to do so requires a shot to the brain, which is about the size of a cantaloupe, while the animal may be charging toward you. Those who choose to attempt this feat usually have someone standing behind them with a .500 H&H (50 caliber), which has the ability to take the animal off his feet with most any direct hit.

Certainly, we're not hunting elephants here, but what is the easiest to shoot, with the least recoil, and may be a cute, little, concealable gun might not be enough knock down a 220-pound "gorilla" who intends to do you harm. We're not hunting here; we're defending, and the cold reality is that should it become necessary, whatever you're using had better be enough to stop your assailant, or we're back to the old "take it off you and shove it where the sun doesn't shine," or worse.

Assume that you've received the appropriate training. You know how to load and unload it, you know where and how to carry it, you have learned how to shoot it, you are ready

Joseph E. Rice

to protect its whereabouts at all times, and you're ready to go.

All you have to know now is whether you are capable of using the gun in a defensive situation. This doesn't mean "I think that I could do it if I had to," this means that you know, without any doubt in your mind, that should you have to defend your life, you are capable of taking the life of your assailant.

Sort of frightening, isn't it? It should be. The right to life is our most sacred possession, both legally, guaranteed in our Constitution, and biblically, "Thou shall not kill." But, you are allowed to take a life to save your own and in defense of another person when his or her life is in danger ... but we aren't making you a vigilante; we're talking about you protecting you.

Here's another truth to remember before you strap on a gun. If you aren't capable of pointing a gun at an assailant that you believe is putting your life at risk, and you aren't capable of pulling the trigger and ending the life of your assailant, don't buy a gun. If you don't believe that you're capable of doing this, don't lose any sleep over it; there are other things to do, just don't consider a firearm.

One of the recurring experiences that I have had in the course of the protection of stalking victims is that, depending on the length of time that the person has been victimized and the seriousness of the incidents that she has endured, her psychological base has been seriously shaken. This isn't to say that she's mentally ill, and without the recent experiences that she has been through, she might be more than capable of properly possessing a firearm, but that isn't the case, and we have to play the hand that we've been dealt. This means

60

that in many stalking cases, introducing a firearm into an already chaotic existence without courting disaster is hoping for circumstances that may not be attainable. The perceived increase in security provided by the weapon may in fact, create a situation that is exactly the opposite.

CHAPTER 9
LEGAL STALKING THROUGH THE COURTS

It is generally recognized that the stalker's most important goal over his victim is that of control. We're all familiar with the serious cases involving individuals who have been victimized to the extent that they were ultimately subjected to acts of violence. Their adversaries were those that either had a limited store of knowledge to draw from, or they were in some degree of mental state that afforded them no degree of concern over the consequences of their acts. However, there is still yet another degree of stalker that exists ... the one who chooses to use completely legal means to destroy his victim. That is the subject of this chapter.

How many times have you known of a couple that has experienced a divorce, and several years after the actual divorce decree, they are still in and out of the courts over financial and property issues? This is an issue of control, not economics. How many times have you heard of a situation in which a divorce has occurred, and for years after, the issue of child custody, sometimes even to the time in which the children are grown enough to make their own choices, has continued? Again, this is an issue of control, not one of welfare for the children. Now, let me make one thing very clear: These two previous examples are not limited to men; many times the women are the aggressors in these cases.

In one of the southern states, a man and his wife set out to sever their "ties that bind." Both were professional people with sizeable incomes. They had two children. The divorce was not a simple one, in that there was a sizable pool of joint assets, and the issues that caused the split were somewhat volatile, but with enough money and enough lawyers, proceed it did, and a final decree of divorce was issued some six years ago. At the time of the divorce, the children were seven and nine years old respectively. Since that time, their mother has remarried, as has their father, and the children are thirteen and fifteen years old.

What is unique about this situation, you say? There is still a frequent and continuing issue over the children, who, in societies of old, could have already been fostering their own families, but even in today's world are old enough to make their own decisions in that state.

In this case, the husband, who never wanted the divorce, has refused to accept the fact that life, as he wished it to be, is over. Even though both parties have remarried, and the children are nearly grown, he cannot and will not allow this to end. Why? If he does, it will finally be over, and he didn't get what he wanted. As long as there is an issue involving any part of the previous marriage, in his mind, he hasn't lost.

The process has been exacerbated by the fact that the husband has been subject to bouts of psychological instabilities, compounded by a relatively ample supply of cash available to fund the next round of legal events.

Let's consider the situation of the former wife in this case. Do we think that she is any less psychologically frazzled than someone who is receiving obscene phone calls or mail, or having everyone talking about her situation? I can tell you that she is not. She is being stalked just as surely as if she were to be followed everywhere that she was to go.

Then what makes the difference in this case? Her "ex" has broken no laws to accomplish any of this.

A client of mine, a professional woman in a Midwestern town, had a relationship with a man for about nine years. During the first four years of the relationship, they resided in an apartment; the remaining years they spent in a residence purchased by my client. Over time, the client began to recognize a variety of personality traits in the man with whom she resided and made the decision to sever the relationship. From several successful years in the business world, the client had a respectable bank account and a very good debt/equity number on her mortgage.

The relationship hit bottom when she had to resort to a protection order to remove him from the house. His parting comment was that he was the last person that she wanted to mess with and that he would destroy her.

It was only a short period of time before the client was notified of a lawsuit filed against her for divorce. Even though they had never married, in the state in which they resided, he sued her under the common law/palimony clause of the law.

Clearly, the evidence showed that he could prove no financial interest in the house or her assets. He did not attend one session of court, and ultimately, the case was decided in her favor. However, the court costs and the attorney fees cost her a sizeable amount of money.

Shortly thereafter, she was notified of a second suit naming her, claiming trust in equity, or trying to say in a second suit what the court said "no" to in the first suit. Again, he did not attend court, and the decision was rendered in her favor, after considerable legal fees. However, the judge did find that the filing of the lawsuit was improper and issued a finding against the plaintiff and issued an order allowing my client to sue the other attorney for bringing the suit.

Just as that case was being settled, her house was selling in an adjoining county. She was notified of a suit filed against her, claiming an interest in her house, encumbering the sale of the house in the pending court case. Eventually, as the case was about to come to trial, a settlement was reached giving her former boyfriend about $10,000. The judgment from the previous case was then used against the plaintiff.

In total, the attorney fees, court costs, and the settlement cost my client nearly $200,000. The plaintiff, her ex, received only $10,000. He got little money, and of that, most of it went to the attorney who represented him. He got all the attorneys to take the cases on contingency by finding "sleazy lawyers" with whom he shared the same ethical standards. It wasn't about money. It was about control. As long as the suits were going on, he believed that it wasn't over; he was controlling her just as he was when they were together.

You should understand that this wasn't all that he did. His antics became quite sadistic. He was ultimately forced to another state because of serious financial obligations. Whenever he was in town or about to come to town, the creditors were confidentially notified of his whereabouts. He finally decided to remain out of town, and his victim is doing just fine today.

Even recognizing the torment imposed and the financial burden placed on my client, he broke no laws. Everything that he did with the courts was legal.

It is not unusual for wounded suitors to use the legal system to tie up the assets, time, and, in general, the life of their prey. It can be accomplished through property issues, support and child custody issues, and any other issue of which the two, once close individuals, were a party.

The overwhelming problem in defending such issues is that your adversary is not intent on winning. You may put on a terrific defense and ultimately win, but only after being subjected to extraordinary delays, legal tactics designed only for the purpose of prolonging the process, and incredible costs. Remember, your "sleaze" has most probably found an attorney with whom his own ethics are on par.

Unfortunately, there isn't much defense to this tactic outside of good legal work. In their zealousness, your sleaze and his sleaze attorney usually create an error somewhere. When that occurs, assuming that you have appropriate counsel, you must take the opportunity and hopefully put your adversary on defense while you take the offensive position. Remember, in these situations, you don't get many opportunities to turn the tables, and when you do, you can't let them get away.

Joseph E. Rice

CHAPTER 10
HOW TO APPROACH THE AUTHORITIES

Approaching the authorities when you find yourself in the position of believing that you might be in harm's way can certainly be a daunting task. This is caused for a variety of reasons.

Most normal folks out there haven't made a habit of being in regular contact with their local police department, and the limited contacts that they may have had in the past were most probably calling for a specific situation that may have already happened or was imminent. Their personal safety was not the focal point of the call.

For instance, if you came home from vacation and found that your home had been burglarized, even though it involved your home and your property, the incident had already occurred, and while you're dealing with the anger that is associated with any such situation, there is no particular anxiety over your personal well-being.

Calling the local authorities for assistance in a protection, stalking, or domestic case presents a different scenario. You're about to call an agency whose job it is to protect you, and you are going to go through an experience not matched since the days of the "inquisitions." To have any chance of being successful in your attempt at securing their help, you will have to, figuratively, "bare your chest and hand them a sword."

69

It will be necessary for you to chronicle in great detail the reasons for your call, the history of the situation, and the activities that have led you to believe that you are in danger. (As we have discussed, this can be somewhat simpler by use of a protection order, but obtaining a protection order requires nearly the same process in front of a judge.)

Now, in fairness to the local "coppers," they cannot, nor should they, take any action against any individual based on inadequate information, and you must keep in mind, you are giving them only one side of the story. You may be the most honest person in the world, and you may be totally accurate in your information, but at the time of your first contact with them, they don't know any of that … so to make any determination without putting you through the ringer would be somewhat irresponsible.

If I am representing a client in a stalking situation, I will handle the first contact with the police. This provides several benefits in that they know that the situation must be serious, they know that you must be serious, and additionally, they're talking to someone from the "brotherhood."

When I come into a case that has already had law enforcement involvement, sometimes the process is more complicated. This occurs for a variety of reasons, the two most common being: a chauvinistic, disinterested, or suspicious attitude on the part of the authorities, or the belief that the victim is "just another nut" because of the number of contacts that have been made for all types of unbelievable reasons. The absolute most common reason is a combination of the two that I have just mentioned.

I would never suggest to any client that she wasn't scared and looking for some form of comfort for that horrible feeling, but the coppers aren't there to listen to all your problems, nor are they your personal advisors. Each call to the police that turns out to be nothing only serves to erode away your credibility ... sort of like the "Little Boy Who Cried Wolf." So, I always give my clients this simple rule: If the house is on fire, call the fire department; if your bad guy is trying to come through the door with an axe like Jack Nicholson in *The Shining*, call the police; anything else, call me! We will discuss the appropriate action calmly, rather than another frantic call to the police department. I always let the authorities know that this is the arrangement that I have with my client, their potential victim, letting them know that "if she calls, it's serious."

It is not unusual that a victim who was perfectly normal prior to the beginnings of a messy divorce or a stalking excursion may begin to exhibit examples of instability before its conclusion. This is certainly not a fault or a weakness; you have never been through anything like this, and it strikes at the very foundation of your stability. It is therefore extremely important that any calls to the police be as composed and collected as possible, recognizing that if someone is chopping through your bathroom door as you make the call, composure may be in short supply.

Occasionally when dealing with the local police, I will get the comment that "she's a nut." Usually it is more productive if I don't challenge their opinions, be they right or wrong, so my usual reply is to ask, "How much of a nut was she before this started?" This usually elicits the response, "We don't know, because we had no dealings with her before all this." At this juncture, I usually query them as to why that is: "Could it be that she was a law-abiding citizen before her world was turned upside down by a possible psychotic criminal?" I will usually follow this up with the comment that we have no measurement of the damage that the situation has caused this person and that the person we see is probably nothing like she was before all this began to happen.

I can recall a case that occurred in an extremely rural area. The victim had been subjected to the antics of her stalker for over a year before any outside help was brought into the scene.

Rebuilding her stature with the state police in the area was nearly impossible due to the number of calls that she had made, the types of activities that she alleged were being done to her by her stalker, and a continual deterioration of her psychological demeanor as time progressed.

The woman was armed anytime that she was on her own property, in her own house, or in her car—the only exception being when she was sleeping, at which time she had a shotgun under the bed. She had cameras and alarms throughout her home and on her property. This case had an equal amount of paranoia and bona fide risk. The bad guy was dangerous, and he had done many of the bizarre things that the state police found hard to believe, but her volume of calls and her demeanor during the calls, added to the bizarre nature of the alleged actions, caused an increasingly strong perception that she was a "nut."

In a discussion with the post commander of the state police barracks that had jurisdiction, I suggested that with all that we (he and I) knew about the situation, not only the bad guy, but also the victim, we would both look pretty stupid if there were to be a homicide at that residence, which I assured him was a distinct possibility ... either her doing him, or him doing her.

The post commander agreed with this logic, and he authorized a night operation to verify if some of the allegations were true. The operation was successful, with the bad guy trying to show four state troopers just how bad he was, resulting in the bad guy presently doing five years in the state penitentiary.

Quite some time ago, most states instituted legislation calling for protection of the victim in any police or court proceedings if she were a victim of rape. These laws are usually referred to as the "rape shield." This was a necessary step in not only the protection of victims, but also the prosecution of rapists. Without some protection from the "investigative beating" and the "defense beating" that victims were subjected to, there would be no prosecutions for lack of victims who were willing to come forward.

This was caused in most part because of a practice of putting the victim on trial—her sexual habits, her past relationships, personal information that was not relative to the fact that she had been forced to have sex with someone. The rape shield has done a fairly good job in quelling the attacks on victims during the investigative process and the subsequent prosecutions, but there is still the incidence of law enforcement trying the victim prior to believing that she has been harmed.

I know that we're not discussing rape in this chapter, but I want to make a point. There is no such protection for a victim in a stalking case, and too many times, the victims are taken lightly—sort of the philosophy that "I can't do anything about that, but if he shoots you, come back in, and I'll investigate the shooting."

It is therefore not unusual for a stalking victim to get the "runaround" when trying to get assistance with her problem. For this reason, a protection specialist can be extremely helpful in getting the coppers on board.

But if circumstances dictate that you must contact the authorities yourself, remember several little hints:

•If you have a protection order, contact the police immediately and give them a copy.

•Provide the answers to as many questions as they may ask and try not to get defensive or angry.

•There is a tendency to believe that any woman complaining about anything that hasn't or isn't spilling her blood is just another scorned woman trying to get revenge. Understand this from the beginning and don't get angry or defensive. Just answer the questions.

•Contact the police sparingly. Remember, any call that does not result in some action being taken just undermines your credibility.

•Compose yourself before you call. Do this by having what you want to say written down, and if you have been upset before you call, wait until you're under control.

•Don't theorize about what you believe has happened. If you have facts, present them. If you have theories, keep them to yourself or offer them to the police only when asked. If you are working with a protection specialist, save your theories for him or her.

•Keep the emotion out of your call. Your bad guy may be your ex-husband, ex-boyfriend, or a stranger. Be cool and matter-of-fact when you describe the facts.

•If the officer that you are talking with doesn't agree with you, don't get angry. This only fuels the perception that this is another "disgruntled woman."

•If you aren't getting satisfaction from whomever you are calling to report the problem, make an appointment with the chief of police (in a small department) or a supervisor (in a larger department) and calmly express your concerns, not complaints.

Remember this, if the treatment that you receive isn't as you would expect, don't go over the edge and succeed in creating a theory that "maybe she's getting what she deserves" from the stalker. Take it slow and keep in mind that you can't change law enforcement organizations like you can change attorneys or doctors. They're the ones that ultimately will have to be your help. Don't get mad and win the battle but lose the war.

Having said all that, most departments and most officers will do all that the law allows them to do to help you if you posture yourself properly. Just keep in mind that they have crimes that have already happened and others that are happening now to deal with, before they can devote great amounts of time to something in which no one was hurt and may or may not happen again ... to say nothing of a potential stalking situation in which no action has occurred.

Just always try to present yourself in your most business-like manner. It makes you seem so much more credible.

CHAPTER 11
HOW TO HIRE AND FIRE AN ATTORNEY

Sometime during the course of your experience as a victim of stalking, there will probably be a need for you to be represented personally by an attorney. Recognizing that should your problem be a serious one, the activities of the stalker are criminal, in which case your attorney is the prosecutor or district attorney. The only problem with representation by the prosecutor is the fact that he or she is also prosecuting murders, rapes, assaults, and armed robberies. It is not unusual that a stalking victim's case falls well down the ladder of importance on the state's list of priorities.

The other problem, as we have touched on previously, is the fact that there is a great deal of activity that the stalker can wreak upon your life that falls below the level of a prosecutable case; therefore, the need for other remedies may exist.

The selection of an attorney can be a difficult one. There are several problems that occur when dealing with these fine representatives of the downtrodden. The first is that, unlike doctors, who, when you tell them of a problem that is not in their realm of expertise, will usually send you to a specialist in that area, some attorneys believe that they are capable of handling any problem that comes through their door. This is further exacerbated by a public that, unlike dealing with a doctor when they demand a specialist, believes that all attorneys are the same. For instance, you wouldn't go to a

77

podiatrist if you had headaches and believed that you had a brain tumor. Attorneys are no different. You can't expect the guy who wrote your mother's and dad's wills or the guy who handled the closing on your house to effectively represent you in a matter that may become as complex as protecting you from a stalker.

Another problem that exists is the lack of a general understanding of the seriousness of the problem that you may be having. There is a pervasive theory among law enforcement that a woman who is complaining about some man that she believes is harassing her may have done something to deserve the treatment that she is getting, or that she is paranoid about whatever she believes is happening and that it isn't that serious, or that she is just trying to get back at the guy for previous treatment that she believes to have been unfair.

Now, I'm not going to tell you that all of these reasons aren't occasionally the case, and I won't tell you that all law enforcement perceives the victim in this manner, but it does occur, and having an attorney that may share those feelings or is sympathetic to the position of the authorities is not only counterproductive, but you're also paying for this lack of effective treatment.

Any attorney that you may choose to represent you would be taking the case as your advocate ... and that means your advocate. Professional courtesy to the opposing counsel should be tempered. Lazy, ineffective law enforcement should not be tolerated, and an appropriate level of attention to your problem should be constant.

Now, it is important to understand that just as the prosecutor has other cases, so does your attorney, and you can't expect that you will receive constant and always-immediate attention. You should understand that constant and repeated phone calls to the attorney's office for "updates on the case" will usually go unreturned, unless of course, there is an update to report, of which you probably already would have been notified.

Whomever you retain is not your psychologist, and he is not going to be your personal counselor, listening to your every problem, but when the need arises, he should be available to deal with the problem in a timely and effective manner. You have every right to expect that whomever you retain will be an effective advocate for you; however, you must conduct yourself appropriately as a client.

There are several theories that may assist you in the selection and continuing relationship with an attorney. One that I have always found to be useful as a measuring stick is that the attorney will never be more attentive to your problem than he was when you were trying to retain him. If it takes you an unreasonable amount of time to get in to see him, you can be assured that his attention to your situation will move at the same or lesser speed.

Another thing to remember when dealing with an attorney is relatively simple, but often not considered. While it is true that he is highly educated and possesses a great deal of power, you are the customer, and he is the provider … he's working for you. Don't you forget that, and don't allow him to forget that.

I can recall a stalking case in which I was involved. The client had been referred to me through her psychologist, and at the time that I entered the case, she had been getting "jerked around" by the attorney who had been handling the sale of her house. This particular stalker had chosen to destroy this woman through a variety of methods, but one that he was using rather successfully was the legal system, through a variety of different lawsuits against the victim. We discussed this in detail in chapter 9, "Legal Stalking Through the Courts."

My client made the decision to fire the attorney that she had used for her real-estate problem and the ensuing lawsuit. She was referred to another attorney by her psychologist. The attorney was an acquaintance of his, and he was sure that this guy was the man for the job. I had just entered the case and attended the initial meeting with the new attorney. There had previously been a deposition scheduled for a date one week from the date of that first meeting. I suggested that since he had only just entered the case, it might be more appropriate to ask for a continuance of the deposition, so that he could familiarize himself with the facts of his new client's case. His reply was that he had known the opposing counsel well for many years, and that since it was already scheduled, he didn't want "to do that to the other attorney." This should have been a clue, but since he was a friend of the doctor, and since he had been highly recommended, we persevered with his game playing and mollycoddling of the other attorney until I recommended that she fire him several months later.

The point is, again, that your attorney is <u>your</u> attorney. His entire purpose is to represent you in the best way possible, and if for any reason, he isn't prepared to do so, he needs to go. Now that I've successfully trashed the legal profession, let me suggest the things that a good, involved attorney can do for you.

All good attorneys who have had experience in criminal or domestic law are more than aware of the things that occur when someone is being victimized and possibly brutalized by another. Given their experience level, they are in a position to deal with the prosecutors. They practice in that arena, they know them, and they are able to have conversations about the things that are occurring to "their client" and let the prosecutor know that one of his brothers or sisters is watching. This doesn't mean that if there isn't a case capable of taking before the courts one will suddenly appear as a favor to your attorney, but it does mean that the officers of the court are aware that the victim is serious and has someone looking out for her.

If the possibility of retaining legal counsel is present, and there may be a particular attorney that either is recognized in the appropriate area of practice or any other reason that would cause you to consider that particular person (either you or someone you trust knows him or her), you should immediately contact that attorney and discuss your problem. The reason for this is that bad guys will often employ a tactic referred to by attorneys as "conflicting them out." What this means is that your bad guy selects the several attorneys that you might consider, then contacts them as though he were going to retain them, talks briefly about "his" side of the events in question, then goes away, without hiring them. Then, that attorney is no longer available to represent you. The reason is that the attorney has talked to the principal on the other side of the case and may have been made aware of circumstances in the case, no matter how little. Even though he was not retained by your bad guy, he now has a conflict in representing you. This is yet one more control tactic.

Certainly, if the need for a protection order is present, a good attorney can prepare it and argue it before the judge. If the incidents have escalated beyond what is appropriate to stop with a protection order, but not to the level of a criminal prosecution, there are actions that can be taken such as lawsuits for harassment, menacing, libel, and slander—none of which are "bulletproof," but given the right stalker, may be another tool to use in stopping his behavior.

The legal system is a complicated maze of different paths. While there is no single direction that can be suggested that works in all cases, a competent, thoughtful, concerned attorney can give the proper guidance so you don't feel like a rat wandering around looking for a piece of cheese.

The appropriate relationship with your attorney is one in which you feel like he is genuinely interested in your well-being and is looking for ways to remedy your problem. Indifference, treatment as an inferior, blaming you for the problem, and suggesting that you should just "be calm" and let things take care of themselves are all signs that you may need to "change pews in this church."

And should that be the case, don't hesitate. If your problem has exacerbated to this level, inattention to the crisis can be dangerous. Do you think that my attorney friend who had two of his clients murdered the same day that they got protection orders would be inattentive to a client who claimed to be the victim of a stalker? I don't think so.

CHAPTER 12
DO YOU NEED A
PSYCHOLOGIST?

Not so many years ago, the thought of someone seeing a therapist was not only somewhat rare, but the situations that most people were aware of—if they even knew of anyone who was seeing a "shrink"—were extreme … not so today, thank goodness!

Today, while you personally may not realize this, seeing a therapist no longer has the social stigma attached to it that it once had. From the use of child psychologists in the schools to adult counseling for a variety of problems, this specialty of medical treatment has become one of the great tools of a somewhat troubled society. Of course, the age-old question pervades … that being whether there are more persons in need of treatment today than in days of yore or is the seeking of help from a therapist just more common today.

I don't believe that there is any question that it is the latter. Years ago, a young man with a somewhat lower IQ, that being in the area of sixty-eight or sixty-nine, would have just been considered "slow" and been relegated to a life of physical labor, possibly farming or something that he could understand with his limited abilities. If he had someone help him with his books and major business decisions, he would be just fine on the farm. Today, that same person would be tested, counseled, educated, and trained to help him become a functioning individual in society, and hopefully, not relegated to only manual labor.

Another example of the societal changes in this area is the school system in Palm Beach County, Florida. It has all the regular high schools in their county. It also has a series of satellite schools, History and Science, School of the Arts, etc., and it also has an inpatient psychological clinic. The clinic is for students in need of such treatment. They can go there for a semester or whatever time necessary determined by the therapist, continue with their studies (since there are teachers assigned to the clinic), and return to their class, without missing a step. While there (it is no secret where a particular student is), their friends correspond with them during their stay, and when they return to class, there is no stigma.

Now, I'm not suggesting that every young person needs to have a "tour of duty" in an inpatient clinic as a part of growing up. The point is that when extensive treatment is necessary, times have changed, and help is available, without anyone having to feel that it is a "cross to bear" for the rest of his or her life. You may be asking yourself how this applies to your situation, so let's see if we can understand how this may apply to you.

What is the primary goal of the stalker, the estranged or former husband, or any bad guy that may be after you? To destroy your psychological stability! Even if your bad guy's ultimate plan might be to harm you physically, it won't be a surprise. The warning signs, the hints, and the discussions with others are all part of a systematic plan to let you know what may be coming. Why? To chip away at you mentally … and this is the guy whose goal of your psychological destruction is secondary. Most of these guys' primary goal is to totally destroy your existence which you once enjoyed. Remember, in their sick minds they believe that somehow, they may be able to force you to believe that you belong with them, and if not, to see to it that no one else wants you or has a chance to be with you.

You are in the worst of psychological situations. You are being attacked in a manner that you have never experienced. Your entire life is being challenged at every turn. Your social life is destroyed; your immediate family life is now destroyed if he was a part of your immediate family, and if not, the remaining family is certainly under extreme duress; your employment may be in jeopardy; and you don't know what to expect next.

All this wonderful "stuff" may be the product of someone you loved and trusted. Usually the bad guy's plan works fairly well, at least initially. Remember, we said that he was your confidant; he knows the intimate details of your life, and he will use them against you. You need to recognize that you haven't spent your waking moments planning how to defend yourself against something like this, but the bad guy may have been, and most probably has been, planning things such as this for quite some time.

If you think back over your time with him, you can probably recognize some of the things that he is using against you in his dealings with others, so what's happening to you now shouldn't be such a surprise. Remember, this isn't about his feelings; this is all about his character, or lack thereof.

I want to stress to you that this is a devastating experience in your life, and understanding that is probably the biggest issue in survival. Seeking appropriate help is nothing more than applying the proper resources to your defense plan. If you begin to lose your stability, putting your ability to make good judgments in question, you will be losing the strongest member of your defense team ... YOU!

Anyone in these types of life situations has a tendency to consider that some degree of blame may be hers and that she wasn't as considerate, caring, understanding, and helpful as she could have been to the bad guy. Maybe so, maybe not, but none of that justifies what she is experiencing.

You are probably a product of your own personality and of a relationship that has systematically convinced you that you are somehow less of a person, certainly less than he is and probably less than most others. This is something that isn't undone overnight—remember that it didn't occur overnight—but it is something that therapy with the proper clinician can assist you in overcoming.

Psychologists practice in many specialty fields. Some are forensic psychologists, dealing with extreme violent crises and the court systems; some specialize in treatment for addictions; some are specialists with children; and some specialize in treatment of abused women and women in crisis. Those who concentrate on women in crisis are the ones that can be most helpful, for is there any doubt that you are in crisis?

But much the same as your attorney, you must determine quickly if the selection that you have made is the proper person to assist you in your problem. Your self-esteem is the number one factor in your ability to protect yourself and get on with your life. If you sense that there is any thought by the doctor you have selected of you fixing the problem with the bad guy, you have the wrong doctor. If there is ever a suggestion of a joint session with you and the bad guy, you have the wrong doctor. Why might this be such a bad thing? Let's see if you have been paying attention. Wouldn't something like a joint session provide more information to your bad guy, to say nothing of putting you in his presence, which should never occur?

Another thing to consider is that if there has ever been any previous counseling by that particular therapist for you and your bad guy or for other family members, in which both of you were involved, find someone else. That therapist is conflicted and should not have any involvement with you and your present situation.

While I am not a psychologist, I can tell you that I have had the experience of working with quite a few of them in stalking and abuse cases. I can also tell you that I have had occasion to refer quite a few of my clients to psychologists, when they had not already sought one themselves, in an effort to help them stabilize themselves so that I could better assist them in their protection. The assistance of the proper clinician is invaluable to you and to anyone such as me that may be trying to help you, and while I won't say that every victim needs the help of a therapist, I will say that most will at some time before the incident is concluded.

Another thing to consider is the fact that a psychologist is an individual whose entire educational experience is centered on human behavior. Should you find yourself under the care of a psychological clinician during this crisis, his evaluation of the experiences that you will be sharing with him can sometimes provide a clinical insight into the bad guy's behavior—either in your description of an individual incident or in his evaluation of a continuing pattern of conduct and behavior. This type of evaluation can become extremely beneficial to the law enforcement authorities, your attorney, your protection specialist, or anyone else who is closely involved in your situation and trying to assist you.

Even though you may be able to work through this crisis without clinical assistance, it is still something that you should consider, even if the crisis has subsided. You have probably been victimized by a friend and confidant. This is the most serious violation of your trust that can occur, and if you don't deal with that fact properly, you may find it affecting you for the rest of your life in any relationships in which you may become involved that require trust.

Remember, "If you don't think you're John Wayne, no one else will," and we just want to use every possible resource available to make sure that this is an issue about which there is no doubt.

CHAPTER 13
PLANNING AN EXIT
STRATEGY

Stalking and abuse incidents most usually are the result of the end of some relationship, real or perceived. When our spoiled, pouting, mamma's boy finds that there is something that he can't have or control that he believes is his God-given right…and when he can't have it he also believes, that absent the fulfillment of his wishes and desires, he has the right to destroy or certainly make life miserable for the one whom he believes is the cause of his unhappiness. After all, his happiness is the most important issue in existence in the free world, and if others' freedom must end to further his pursuit of happiness, well, that's just the way it has to be.

Now, certainly the battered women's organizations across the country do a great job when they get the chance, and I wholeheartedly support their efforts. However, what we are trying to accomplish in our discussions throughout this book is directed toward avoidance of the situation that results in a battered woman.

Accordingly, any situation that is now or may in the future threaten your safety, security, or general well-being will ultimately require you to extract yourself from harm's way.

So, where do you begin? Let's start with a simple philosophy that you should record indelibly in your mind. As you begin to plan your departure, continually remind yourself of the obnoxious, demeaning, demanding, overbearing, abusive, and violent behavior that you have witnessed or of which you have been a victim. Each time you revive these thoughts in your mind, consider how the one who has done all these wonderful, manly, gentlemanly, considerate things will react when you take some action that will be immediately perceived as an assault on his manhood. If you want a program that details what to expect from this guy, just look back at what you've already experienced and assume the same type of behavior, only you should magnify it several times.

Simply said, if he was a "jerk" when he believed that he had complete domination over you, what makes you think that he will be any better when you "challenge the kingdom" in which he resides. Trust me, he won't be any better! Now, to suggest that all this creates an environment from which you can never remove yourself is not correct. All I am saying is that it requires an "exit strategy," or a plan for your departure.

Let's begin with where you will go. At least initially, it's a good idea to land somewhere where there are other people. Remember what we said previously: Keep him and his acts out in the open, in the sight of others. If he chooses to continue the behavior that you have already witnessed, let him do it in a situation in which the entire world will get the "pleasure" of experiencing just what a great guy he is.

When considering a place to land, usually family or friends will come to mind. You need to keep in mind that in either of these two suggestions, they too have probably had experience with your bad guy; however, their experience may not have been similar to yours. Simply said, their perception may be that your bad guy is a great guy. These individuals are great thespians when it comes to making others think they're nice guys and that you're the problem.

This isn't always the case. Your family and friends may have already been made aware of the situation, either from your telling them or from firsthand experience by witnessing or being involved in one of your crisis situations.

Most of us don't care to "air our dirty laundry," so to speak, for the entire world. First, the situation in which you find yourself tends to be somewhat embarrassing. Almost every woman that I have ever worked with in one of these cases has said, at some time or another, "I just don't understand how or why this is happening to me."

Consider this type of problem in the context of a medical problem. I can tell you personally that having a colonoscopy holds the very last position on my personal list of things I want to do when I get up tomorrow, but it certainly beats cancer of the colon. In female terms, while I don't know this personally, I'm sure most women would prefer a pelvic exam over ovarian cancer.

If your situation has deteriorated to this level, you are in a dangerous position. You cannot afford to have any question about whom you trust. I have told you that you must take steps to protect yourself, and you must! You are the only one who can assume that responsibility. So, when you take others into your confidence, you must weigh the importance of having help against the risk of creating that confidence.

This is one of those situations in which I'm saying to you that good, loyal help is a strong benefit, but you must be sure with whom you are trusting your secrets and your safety.

Sometimes you can determine the mood and mental position of your friends and family by beginning to let

91

out information about your situation prior to your ultimate action. This accomplishes two things. Your action isn't a total surprise, and you have an idea of what type of support you will have from family and friends.

I had a friend who was involved in a marriage that was headed downhill. It seemed that all was well to those who knew him and his wife, until they were alone, and then it was a different situation. Suffice to say that she was not the same person that their family and friends had come to know. She was extremely close to his family and not so close to her own, and because of that, they thought that she could do no wrong, even to the point of believing that the problem was their own son.

This, by the way, is not that unusual. There are frequent situations in which the family loyalty goes to the in-law spouse rather than the blood relative. This is not to suggest that this isn't occasionally the appropriate place for that loyalty, but it should be founded in fact.

Finally, when it became time for my friend to leave, and he began taking the heat from his own family, it was his sister that seriously admonished him over the fact that he had not made the situation known to his own family. She told him that they only had one side of the story and asked him, "What did you expect us to believe?"

It is normal to want to protect your privacy, but these situations are different. The support of those with whom you choose to associate during this crisis must be on your team. This is an issue in which there can be no wavering. If someone close to you has developed a relationship with you and your bad guy, and they don't want to "choose between you," they have to go. It's that simple. If they don't believe you without question and are willing to help you, it's okay, that's their choice. If they won't choose, on your behalf, then they must not believe what you have told them. If they don't believe you, if they don't believe that your bad guy is capable of doing the things that you have told them, get out of there and don't look back. They aren't loyal to you and all they will ever be is a conduit, or worse, in providing information to the bad guy.

Situations obviously vary from case to case, and it is necessary to consider anything that we discuss in general terms, unless I suggest something by beginning with "you can count on," or "don't think for a minute," or something similar. These are points that I am trying to share with you that do not change.

Now, if you happen to be planning your exit in contemplation of a divorce, my first suggestion to you is to retain your attorney prior to taking any overt action. An attorney can help guide you through some of the plans that you should make before you "fire that first shot over the bow." Once you've done that, the battle may be on, and you may not have the opportunity for any long-range planning.

If you are not married to your bad guy, then you will have to make the best plans that you can on your own. Most of the things that we discuss are general areas of life-sustaining necessities, so let's go through a few of them:

•We've already discussed a place to live. Whether it's with a relative, a friend, or on your own, the arrangements should be made as much in advance of your move as possible, as long as you're comfortable that your plans will be kept in confidence. Wherever you intend to reside, your safety is important, so if you are alone, you need to consider the security of your location. If you are with other people, you need to be sure that they are prepared to support your safety should the occasion occur. When you select a location, there should be no reason whatsoever that your bad guy would have for going there. You should also consider the availability and accessibility of law enforcement to whatever location you select.

•Financial considerations are always important. You should quietly be developing a separate financial plan. This means applying for credit in your name, if you don't already have it, setting up your own checking account, and being able to separate any joint obligations that you may have. (Even if you are not married, an attorney may be helpful in some of these financial areas.) Remember, any of these arrangements that you may be making will require confidentiality, so you need to be sure that the bank or any credit company has a different address for you and is aware not to contact you at your old address or telephone number.

•Transportation is an obvious necessity. If you do not have a car accessible to you that you can take when you go, this is another arrangement that you need to make. Your mobility is an absolute necessity.

•Your place of employment is always a touchy situation, but it is necessary that you consider it in your plan. Your employer has volumes of information about you, and unless told differently, that information occasionally can be leaked to the wrong persons. If you have had a relationship for a period of time and your employer or fellow employees are aware of that person's existence, it can provide the opportunity for information to be released. You must be sure that there is no release of information to anyone other than you or your designee.

• We talked about joint obligations. You should not forget benefits. If the bad guy is involved in any of your insurance coverage, or if you are on his, this needs to be taken care of immediately. You should also review any beneficiaries that you may have on any of your insurance or retirement plans and make sure that you have the name designated that you would want to receive your benefits.

• Your minister, priest, or rabbi should be aware of what is occurring. They all have a way of wanting everyone to love each other, and in their attempts at doing right, they can involuntarily create a risk to you. Remember, they're bound by privilege, so you can feel free to talk to them. If you have one of those who happens to believe that you should "work things out at all costs," change churches. (Actually, you should consider this anyway if your bad guy has attended church with you or knows where you go. Remember what we said about being a target of opportunity by being in the same place at the same time? This goes for churches too.)

• Anyone who is close enough to you that they might feel comfortable talking to your bad guy should be aware of your situation as soon as you take some action, to be certain that they don't inadvertently release information without realizing what they are doing.

What we are suggesting here is not all inclusive, but these are some of the more critical areas that will need your attention. What I am trying to do is to get you to think in terms of protecting yourself. As you contemplate your actions, systematically consider each and every issue necessary for you to exist, go through them one by one, and make a list of each of those areas. After doing so, review each of those areas and consider how you can accomplish each totally on your own, excluding any involvement with your bad guy. Once you've made your list, it will then help you to determine your timetable, assuming that you have any time to prepare your departure.

I've told you before that you are the primary person in your safety. What I want here is to see you laying out your plan before the battle begins, while your head is clear and it can be done on your schedule.

Most of these thugs and bullies are just that, and the last thing that they will be expecting is for you to out-think them. Remember, he believes that you're incapable of existing without him, so let him believe that while you quietly plan your departure. Never forget that it's only important what you think of you. What he thinks of you, your talents, abilities, intelligence, and general acumen for self-sufficiency, isn't important ... so let him think that you're helpless. His arrogance, cockiness, self-absorption, and underestimation of you are the best tools that you have with which to undo his domain.

CHAPTER 14
STALKING BY A SUPERVISOR
IN THE WORKPLACE

Throughout this book, we have discussed a variety of methods that any potential adversary of yours might attempt in his process of dominating your life. While those methods vary from person to person and case to case, there is one central theme in all of their activities … that of control and domination.

That being the case, stalking in the workplace—or said in more direct "legal" terms, sexual harassment—can be an extremely devastating situation. On the surface, this should be no great surprise; however, if you've been following our discussions throughout the previous chapters, can you now begin to understand why this can be so devastating and difficult with which to deal?

As we examine most of the methods that you may employ to protect yourself from unwanted contacts, advances, and general activities designed to accomplish the goals of the bad guy, where do we begin? Haven't we said that the most important posture is to eliminate contact and the free-flow of personal information? This is nearly impossible in the workplace if the bad guy happens to be your superior. Remember the definition of your bad guy as "your superior," and I will explain why that is so important shortly.

If you remain in the workplace, you are a captive "target of opportunity." It is difficult for you to totally avoid being in his presence, talking with him, answering his questions, and, depending on your job, possibly being alone with him. So, what we are seeing is that most of the standard defense processes that we may choose to employ may not be appropriate in this arena.

There are three primary issues that must be considered in a potential sexual harassment case. The first is understanding that you are being harassed, if it rises to the level of your taking action to defend yourself and actually making the decision to take some action and proceeding.

There are many degrees of sexual harassment, some of which could be considered by some to be "harmless" (a definition usually suggested by the perpetrator or some other party that has never been involved in such a situation), to the obvious coercive and threatening situations, of which most everyone is familiar.

Let's start with one of the most obvious ... that of either employment security or employment advancement in return for sexual favors. That's pretty obvious. If you don't give me what I want, or "put out," your job may be in jeopardy, or if you do cooperate with my desires, you will be rewarded with advancement in your career.

Let's go to the other extreme: "That's a lovely dress that you're wearing today," accompanied by observations that travel from your face to your ankles and back to your face; referring to you as his "girl," suggesting that you as a woman are inferior to him as a man; the continual request that you perform menial, demeaning tasks that are not part of your job description; the continual discussion of sexual matters; the continual use of obscene language; or conduct in general that causes you to be uncomfortable as a woman in the presence of "your superior" or other males in the workplace.

Now, under the United States Department of Justice (DOJ) federal descriptions of sexual harassment, these examples all match the criteria for sexual harassment. So, should you take action the next time you hear an "off-color" story? Probably not, but I want you to understand that these are the extremes under the federal law.

The next issue is to consider the seriousness of the experience that you are having. Certainly, if you are in the throws of the first example suggested, probably your only choices are to either leave or take some type of action. If your situation is one of the latter, you need to give serious thought to just how badly your comfort level has deteriorated and if it is worth the trauma, risk, and expense dealing with it may bring to you.

You must remember that the harassment laws were not designed to make every man in the workplace a "nice guy." They were designed to protect individuals who are in a "subordinate" and possibly "coercive" environment.

Remember when we talked about this guy being "your superior"? In the laws that are designed to protect you, that term is most important. Its connotation is exactly as you would believe. The bad guy is, by job description, "your superior." This, by definition, creates a subordinate relationship for you with him. The law says that the existence of that relationship cannot be violated. Simply said, his superiority over you is limited to issues contained in your job description. So, unless this guy has somehow wangled into your job description that you are to sexually gratify him, and you've accepted the job, he's way out there in "left field." He is in violation of federal law.

Think about laws protecting juvenile women from sexual activity with adult males. There is an example that may help explain this legal philosophy. Can the most intelligent, mature, and physically developed fifteen-year-old young woman legally consent to sexual intercourse with a twenty-one-year-old man? Absolutely not! The reason is that the law has determined that no matter how mature and intelligent she may be, the twenty-one-year-old adult will hold superiority over her, creating a situation in which undue influence may be exerted. So, if your boss "wants" you, and you are hesitant to resist or say no, can you see the similarity?

In cases that can be proven involving a superior coercing or forcing a subordinate to have sexual activity, the superior is indefensible. However, you should understand that to exercise your rights under this law, you will be subjected to examination not unlike that of a rape victim of years ago. If you remember, we talked about the "rape shield" laws. Well, there isn't any of that type of protection for a sexual harassment complainant.

Recognize here that I would never suggest that any woman subject herself to an existence in a harassing, demeaning, dangerous situation if the situation has risen to that level. What I will suggest is that serious consideration be given to just exactly how "bad" things are before you "fire that first shot over the bow." Embroiling yourself in un-provable allegations or challenging activities that may not seem to be as serious to others, and that are happening to others, need to be seriously reviewed before you "jump into this skillet."

DON'T LET THE BASTARDS BEAT YOU!

Is this type of activity wrong? It is, but we're not trying to fix the whole world here. We're only trying to help you protect yourself. So, if you take this chapter to mean that you should go after your supervisor or your employer because of a bad joke or some bad language, you're missing the point.

Should your situation be one of the more serious issues that need action taken to defend you and your employment, the first thing that should be done is the retention of an appropriate attorney. Not the guy that wrote your will, but an expert in the field of sexual harassment litigation.

An attorney should be consulted in any issue of sexual harassment prior to any action that you may contemplate, regardless of the level of harassment. The reason for this is twofold. There are a variety of remedies available under the DOJ. For instance, any complaint of sexual harassment must be investigated by the company. It may not be resolved to your satisfaction, but it must be investigated. In some of the less serious examples that I have cited, there may be a process that you can follow, but before you begin, you should have counsel. In the more serious examples referred to, there is no doubt that once called to the company's attention, they will "circle the wagons" by immediately turning the issue over to their corporate attorneys. You as an individual are not equipped to compete with a battery of corporate counsel with unlimited resources, so you will then need to retain counsel. Do not be foolish enough to believe that anyone there has your best interests at heart. Their sole purpose is to protect the company and handle damage control. You are the "damage" that they intend to control. If your company happens to be one with a conscience and a heart, that's great, and you can learn of that when your attorney hands you a settlement check and tells you that they're a wonderful, caring, considerate bunch.

I have always subscribed to the theory that if you are going to ultimately need a specialist in some particular field, such as an attorney, or an investigator, retain that specialist first. Why wait until everyone has trampled through the case like Sherman through Georgia, and then request assistance from your attorney? Not only does your attorney then have to represent your interests, as he would have anyway, he may now have to do it by following the script that has been chosen by your adversaries. If you seek counsel prior to any action at your place of business, the entire process will follow the plan laid out by your counsel, not theirs.

CHAPTER 15
THINGS TO AVOID

Certainly the types of dysfunctional interactions between individuals that we have been discussing in this book are the stuff of which great gossip is made. If you were able to somehow deal with your situation privately and confidentially, one of the many traumas of the crisis would be nonexistent, but we know that this is not possible.

We have discussed the need for selected individuals to be aware of the activities in which you now find yourself, not only to provide support, but also so that they don't inadvertently provide the wrong information to the bad guy and to be another set of eyes and ears for you in your attempts to protect yourself. And so, those persons, whomever you choose, are also aware that this is a necessary part of your defense.

Where we need to draw the line is in the interaction between you and those not intimately involved with your crisis. It is not unusual to want to talk about what you are going through. This is a mental defense mechanism; besides, you may find someone who has also experienced what you are going through, or maybe you'll find someone who has some idea of what you might be able to do to alleviate some of your problem.

I'll be benevolent here and suggest that in most of these cases, whomever you are talking to has only your best interests in mind and no ulterior motive whatsoever. That's what I'll suggest ... You make your own decision.

I want to divide the persons about whom I am referring into several basic groups: friends, attorneys, law enforcement officials, and male friends. Obviously, you could experience variations or combinations of these. There are other groups of which you should be aware, but these that I have stated are the basics.

Friends are truly looking out for your best interests; unfortunately, you are most probably hanging on by a thread, depending on the type, duration, and seriousness of your problem. You are therefore vulnerable to any information that you may hear, and when this occurs, there are two rules that you should apply to the information that is given so freely:

- First, if a person hasn't been through a stalking situation, they have no comprehension of what is happening to you and no ability whatsoever to suggest anything that would help you deal with the problem.

- Second, even if your friend has experienced something similar to your situation, remember, all the bad guys are different. They have core deficiencies and traits that may be similar from stalker to stalker, but the individual application of their tactics is specific. Your friend's problem may have been similar, but without every detail, which you will not have, you cannot possibly determine if their experience would be of any help to you. I know that some of these people mean well, but this isn't where you should be getting your guidance.

Attorneys can do wonders for you, assuming two things: that your problem is in their area of expertise and that you have retained them.

The only attorney that you should be "unloading on" is one that you have retained. I have experienced a variety of situations in which a "friend of the family" or "my best friend's boyfriend" or, my personal favorite, "an attorney that I met at a bar last night" have been the principal players. Let me tell you that if any of these "jokers" were worth anything, their response to you would be condolences and a suggestion that you make an appointment in their office to discuss your problem. Ego is a terrible thing, and you have no emotional capacity for anyone that is using you to bolster their feelings.

> •Don't discuss your case with any attorney that you have not hired. The family friend, the girlfriend's boyfriend, and the guy in the bar aren't "in the game." They have nothing to lose, such as reputation or professional liability for doing a bad job.

Law enforcement officials who may cross your path, for any number of reasons, either socially or in a business situation, want to help you in your hour of need. After all, aren't they there to protect and serve? There are immense processes of investigation and snooping that can be undertaken by law enforcement, such as the use of the National Crime Information Center (NCIC) computer network for the purpose of obtaining criminal background information on your bad guy. It's a good tool, but if they aren't officially working your case, it's illegal.

This is a good place to insert one of my basic rules that I live by in the operation of my business and that I always pass on to my clients who are in situations such as yours. If anything is illegal for you to do, it's illegal for you to have someone else do it … and if something that someone does for you is illegal, and you have knowledge, it's the same as if you had personally taken part in the wrongdoing.

Coppers have great egos. I know; I have been part of "the brotherhood" for most of my working life. This isn't a bad thing, for to accomplish many of the heroic ventures that one who has taken an oath to protect others may encounter sometimes requires that near-superhuman, and if not, certainly extraordinary, dimensions occur, dimensions in which mere mortals with normal egos are not adequate. The downside to all of this heroism and superhuman activity is that when not being called upon to perform those incredible feats, most in law enforcement have a tendency to be meddlers, and a meddler in your problem, who has no official capacity to act, is a situation from which no good can come.

>•Any person in law enforcement who is either giving you advice or looking into any aspect of your problem should be in the jurisdiction of your problem and have an ability to act in an official capacity regarding your problem. If not, he should be keeping his ideas and his inquiries to himself. Accordingly, you should be keeping your experiences and your thoughts to yourself. Remember that in most cases his advice is given in an effort to impress someone, namely you, and the last thing that you need to add to your situation is more male ego.

The last category is that of the male acquaintance or friend. The only ego larger than that of a copper is that of a man on the "prowl." Generally, any personality mode that will accomplish the slightest degree of impression on his prey (that is usually you) is acceptable behavior. Now, I will allow the benefit of the doubt here in that every male has a particular style for "the chase," but what I will not allow for is the possible danger that can be done to you and your situation by one of these "jokers" who just doesn't realize the danger of your predicament or just how psychologically fragile you may be at the time of the encounter with this "knight in shining armor." Obviously, you're just another "damsel in distress," and he's here to save you. You can avoid most of this by keeping your situation to yourself, but if you have not, then there he is to save you.

This has been a problem more than once in the course of cases that I have handled involving stalking victims. One in particular involved a client who had met a young man who had developed an interest in her. She had casually discussed her situation with him, and of course, he was ready to jump in and help—never mind the fact that she had paid considerable sums of money to have a protection specialist and attorneys dealing with her problem for months proceeding. This guy knew better. All that he wanted was a date of birth and a social security number, just so he could check the bad guy out. After some heated discussion, it was decided that if that information were to be provided to this guy, he could undertake the remainder of the protection of this client, for I would no longer continue. Was this my ego speaking? No, it was my judgment that nothing legal could be obtained on her behalf by that guy, and I would be no part of that, and if she wanted me to remain on the case, neither would she provide anything to her new acquaintance.

Sometimes it's hard to comprehend just how the law works, but really, it's very simple. If you provide any of the "tools" to anyone who acts in any way, legally or illegally, you are a part of that act. When you have only known someone for a brief period of time, you can't possibly know all that you should know about his character before trusting him with yours, so don't!

  •When a male acquaintance suggests that he can help, don't buy into it; you may be buying into a conspiracy of some illegal act.

These are not the only issues that you should beware of in your dealings with others who are not part of your problem, but these are some of the more frequent situations in which you may find yourself. It isn't that anyone knowingly wants to contribute in any way to your situation, which is already complicated enough, but knowingly or not, providing suggestions or "helping" in a situation in which the individual has no official involvement is reckless in the least and dangerous at most.

Once again, avoidance of these situations is totally under your control. If you can avoid the temptation to talk to someone who seems to be interested but has no personal or professional involvement in your problem, then the examples that we have discussed, and many others of a similar nature, will be nonexistent. There is no doubt that it is difficult to not discuss things with someone who seems to have a genuine interest, especially considering that the environment in which you have been existing lends itself to the need for interaction with others, and obviously, the situation in which you now find yourself is certainly a great topic of discussion ... but just don't do it. Nothing good will come from this type of activity.

CHAPTER 16
SHOULD YOU HIRE A PRIVATE INVESTIGATOR OR PROTECTION SPECIALIST?

Given my particular field of endeavor, my answer to this question should be somewhat predictable. Certainly the administration of your problem by a specialist in the field, not unlike a general contractor on a construction project, can be extremely beneficial. But as we have always said, cases vary, and while some can survive without a myriad of outside help, others may be extremely dependent on that same help in order to fashion an acceptable conclusion.

The discussions that we have had in this book are in no way intended to be the ultimate solution for anyone whose existence is under attack, but rather an explanation of what this problem is, the things that can and usually do occur, and to a limited degree, suggestions on methods to employ that may assist in some situations.

Individuals who specialize in this type of case can come from primarily two areas of practice: that of executive protection (bodyguards) and the area of general background investigation. While one of these examples specializes in immediate protection of the individual, the other spends more time trying to investigate the history of the bad guy. You need the best of both of these examples.

Anyone who is competent in these disciplines probably has some background in law enforcement. To suggest that anyone you may hire will be directing the authorities is incorrect. However, depending on the elapsed time and the stalker's activities, the perception of you at the local police station may need a bit of "brushing up!" This is probably the first place that any specialist should begin. Not only can he or she spend a little time repairing your persona with the "gendarme," it also let's them know that you are serious and willing to accept some responsibility for, and ready to become involved in, your own defense.

As we have discussed before, the single most important part of your safety and security is you. Should you become so unstable that you are no longer able to make intelligent decisions and provide clear and intelligent information to those who may be in a position to help you, your self-defense becomes extremely tenuous. A person whose responsibility is that of protecting others in these situations can be an extremely valuable asset for several reasons.

First of all, you aren't hiring a 400-pound gorilla to walk around and protect you; you're hiring someone who has immensely more experience than you in this field. You aren't hiring someone who is a sharpshooter; you are hiring someone who will help you avoid being in a situation that would ever require a weapon.

What you are hiring, hopefully, is the brains and experience of someone who will be able to apply his or her knowledge and experience to this crisis situation, coolly, calmly, and without emotion. You are hiring someone who knows his way around law enforcement and the courts. As we have said, your personal reputation may have become somewhat tarnished with the authorities. If you have the appropriate person representing you, he will have the ability to restore the law enforcement's confidence in you and the seriousness of your problem.

The appropriate person will be able to independently investigate the circumstances that you have been experiencing and be able to provide any assistance to the authorities in the further resolution of your case.

The appropriate person will be able to assist you in your own personal security and safety. This is usually in areas of physical security of your home and workplace, your travel habits, your personal activities, the screening of individuals that you should be wary of in their relationship to your bad guy, and the issues that may pertain to the purchase, licensing, training, and use of firearms.

Generally speaking, you aren't hiring a bodyguard as much as you are hiring a personal security consultant. As a non-family member and not one of your friends, this is an individual who has the ability to observe and make recommendations on issues of your safety and security without being personally or directly connected to any of the persons or issues involved.

All of this can be extremely helpful, assuming that you have the proper person and can afford the services.

Joseph E. Rice

CHAPTER 17
INDIRECT HARASSMENT

When someone chooses a course of action bent on destroying another's personal existence, it requires a plan ... and quite frighteningly, his plan is usually quite well thought out and intricate. Your goal needs to be that of anticipating, as best as possible, those things that may occur and try to be prepared to negate the effects of any action intended to turn your life upside down.

Obviously, the bad guys of the world all possess certain of the same character traits, and their ability to formulate "plans of attack" is no exception. Simply said, they are all creatures of opportunity. Their success is dependent on opportunities they may discover that allow them to get into your life and use those situations to whatever means they find appropriate to accomplish their goal. What works for one stalker against his victim may not work with another stalker and victim, as the circumstances necessary may not exist. But the common thread is that of persistence in search of any weakness that may create an opportunity to implement their plan.

Victims, too, have a common denominator: that of vulnerability. Diffusing the plans of a stalker can also have a common thread: that of preparedness. If an intended victim is anticipating certain disruptive actions and takes whatever steps necessary to combat those actions, the damage from those actions will be at least minimized, if not completely negated.

To give examples of every type of harassing action that these guys can come up with would create an anthology to

113

rival several volumes of *War and Peace*, and most probably, by the time that information went into print, those who concentrate on destroying others' lives would have come up with some new versions that wouldn't have made print. So, we aren't going to cover everything, but I'm going to give a few examples of the types of actions that can occur.

In one situation, the victim lived in a rural setting on a piece of property that had considerable value. The experience that she had endured had existed for some time before she obtained any type of professional help.

Her adversary was an individual who had a considerable history with the courts involving proven and suspected violent behavior, enhanced by an increasing degree of mental instability. Even though she was acting basically alone in her defense during that time, she had recognized the necessity to remove herself from the area.

She had contacted several realtors and listed her property for sale. There seemed to be a reasonable degree of interest, and there were several individuals who expressed a desire to make an offer on the property, but the interest soon waned. Finally, after several of these occurrences, one of the realtors told her that prospective buyers were being driven off by the individual who had been stalking her. He would, through a variety of means, find a way to contact the interested parties and provide an extremely colorful description of the current property owner and a history of the activities at the property, and ultimately convince them that this was not the property that they should purchase.

Realistically, the prospective buyers probably weren't deterred as much by the stories as they were horrified by the storyteller. She soon found out that all of the neighbors in the surrounding rural area were aware of his version of the story, and obviously, his version was totally his perception of the situation. This exacerbated the problem with prospective buyers in that any type of information that they tried to obtain about the neighborhood was tainted with details of the problems that were occurring. Ultimately, the stalker began harassing realtors, to the point that it even became hard for the victim to retain a firm to represent her in the attempts to sell.

Was her stalker harassing or attacking her directly? No! Was he personally threatening her safety or security? No! Was he in violation of the protection order against him? In a strict interpretation, probably not! Was he still stalking her? You bet he was!

Eventually, the bad guy deteriorated even further in his actions, and ultimately, with professional protection help and the state police, he was "squired off" to a much more appropriate place for him to reside, complete room and board, paid for by the state, with an intended stay of about five to seven years.

A young lady met a man through her employment. He seemed like a nice enough guy, and after several personal encounters and enough discussion to generate some degree of interest, he asked her to go out on a date, and she accepted.

The first date was not particularly memorable, but there was no particular problem … she just wasn't too excited about this guy. When he asked her for a second date, she thought that in fairness she should go out with him again, to make sure that it just wasn't her mood the night of the first date.

During the second date, he began talking about his future, and as he talked, she recognized that she was in his plans. The evening ended cordially, and upon arrival at her residence, she thanked him and politely told him that she believed that they should not see each other again socially, though they could still be friendly when they encountered each other at work, but no more dates! He seemed to take it well, and the evening ended.

A week or so had passed, and she was asked out by someone else. They had a lovely evening and, at the end of the date, agreed to see each other again. She did not hear from him again.

While waiting on the call that never came, she met another young man, and they agreed to see each other socially. Once again at the end of the evening, they agreed to see each other again. When a week had passed, and she had not heard from him, she began to wonder what was occurring.

Again, time passed without a call. But, after about two weeks, she received a call from her most recent suitor. He told her that he was embarrassed that he had not called, apologized, and began to explain why. He said that when he had left her home that night after their date, he was confronted by a man on the street outside her apartment complex. The man identified himself as an individual who had been in a long-term relationship with the young lady. He stated that they had just been having some problems and that the young man (her new date) probably didn't want to get involved in the situation as the current situation (his estrangement from the young lady) was only temporary.

The young man apologized for not calling sooner but, nevertheless, expressed his intentions not to call again, as he had no desire to be involved in such a situation. Even though he knew that the story was not true, the fact that another man was interfering with the woman's social life was enough to deter him from getting involved.

I suppose the young man was probably already suffering from a relative lack of interest in the young lady, but regardless of his interest in continuing the relationship, an encounter with someone who may be unstable, violent, or both did very little to enhance his interest in continuing with any type of relationship.

Did the former boyfriend threaten the girl directly? No! Did he physically harm her? No! Was she in imminent danger during this time? Probably not! So, did the stalker break the law? No, probably not. Even if there had been a protection order in place, his indirect contact with individuals who would not have been named on the order most probably would not have violated the order, but there is no question that his actions were intended to disrupt and control her life. Was she being stalked? Absolutely!

In another situation about which I am familiar, the stalker had been friendly with the family of the victim. He had been a part of the normal family outings and had participated as a guest of the brother-in-law, a businessman, in company-related events.

When all went bad, he not only chose to assail the victim, but he also chose to attack the business activities of the brother-in-law. In one instance, extremely damaging information was provided about alleged improper business practices between the family company and its largest client. This information could have had devastating effects had any of it been true.

So, was this illegal? Overwhelmingly. Was there a legal remedy that would have been appropriate for that which had been done? There certainly was. Was anything done? Not a thing! This brings up another issue, and that is whether those around you, those who are attempting to help you and be part of your team, are ready to become actively involved in defending you. In the situation just discussed, the relative of the victim chose not to embroil his business in the process that was already underway involving the victim.

What he failed to realize was that he, too, and his company were separately involved in their own degree of victimization. Even though this was the only run the stalker took at the family company, he was extremely fortunate.

It is not unusual for these guys to attack the victim's place of business. Situations in which attempts are made to contact employers and apprise them of negative information involving their employee (the victim) are not uncommon. Or, should the victim own her own business, it is not uncommon for the stalker to contact customers, again, in an attempt to disperse negative information about the victim.

Sometimes that indirect approach is the method of choice in that it provides the opportunity to accomplish the mission without contact with the victim, thus providing a sense of security for the bad guy. Remember the quote, "Their purpose can't stand the light of day!"

These can be difficult situations to deal with for several reasons. Sometimes information provided to those who may ultimately be the recipients of the negative information from the stalker can be beneficial; however, there is usually a degree of resistance to the dissemination of a personal situation to others. Unfortunately, though, information to others, in advance of the stalker's, is one of the quickest methods of diffusing the situation.

Sometimes a partial attempt at providing, not information, but directions, can be effective. For instance, you could let primary customers be aware that they should only be dealing with you personally, that you've experienced some problems, and that you personally will be handling any contact involving them. In the employee-employer situation, there is no question that you should make your situation known. Not only does this protect you, but it allows your employer to protect others who may inadvertently get in the way. (Don't concern yourself with negative actions toward you by your employer, as there are laws that protect against those things.)

Now, accomplishing all of this is predicated on your being able to explain your predicament without "coming off like a nut," but then again, this is one of the reasons that you want to remain as stable as possible.

Many of the practices employed by the stalker can be predicted by a professional who has experience in this arena because of past experiences with other victims. But, even with that assistance, not every possible scenario will be familiar. And while every particular scenario cannot be predicted, the fact that a scenario may be tried is predictable. You cannot always predict what act may occur, but you can predict that some act will occur. So, the most important posture of defense is that of awareness and preparedness. Anticipating the attempts of acts against you immediately puts you one step in front of your adversary, as he is counting on the element of shock and surprise.

CHAPTER 18
WHAT CAN OCCUR

As we have discussed, there are a variety of methods that can be employed to thwart the efforts of a stalker. Obviously, they vary from case to case, based on the particular circumstances. The instances that follow in this chapter are examples of real-life stalking situations and the results that have occurred. As we have discussed before, the locations and the circumstances have been altered enough to eliminate the possibility of being recognized by anyone who is familiar with the actual case, but the general descriptions of the situations are factual.

A young couple from the northeast had known each other for several years. They were each a part of a group of friends that regularly socialized together, and they too had become close friends. The young lady was romantically involved with another of the male members of the group. After several years, they ended their relationship. It was at this time that she and her current partner became involved romantically, soon moving to marriage and a child on the way. The previous male friend faded into the sunset.

As the new relationship developed, the young lady was approached by the best friend of her former partner, also a member of the group of friends, and advised that since his friend, her previous partner, was out of the picture, there was no longer an impediment to the two of them being together. He stated how he felt about her and indicated that he was sure that she felt the same way. She immediately made it clear that she did not feel the same and attempted to

121

dismiss him. This was the beginning of a long and traumatic stalking affair.

The wounded suitor began a series of increasingly more frightening letters, photographs, and artwork—all depicting situations involving the two of them and his intended life together with her. This was culminated with comments and an act that suggested that the child that she was carrying was his (even though they had never been together sexually), and a threat to the safety of the baby.

The couple sought the assistance of an attorney, who assisted them in obtaining a restraining order. Shortly thereafter, I was contacted and entered the case. The first action undertaken was to do an extensive background on the individual. It was determined that he possessed psychological deficiencies that he had experienced since his early teenage years. His writings and his artwork were reviewed by a forensic psychologist, and the psychologist confirmed that he possessed the psychological traits of someone who could possibly act out his threats.

Personal contacts were made with the authorities in the primary locations where the newlyweds resided and spent most of their time, explaining the seriousness of the situation and providing them with copies of the restraining order and all other background information. Their understanding of the problem and their willingness to respond, basically, without question was assured. A complete security system was installed in the home of the victims, with direct alarm access to the local law enforcement.

Once the young couple was more secure in their setting, it was determined to wait and watch the individual, rather than to confront him. After several months, there was an indication of an incident involving the stalker and another woman that he had met only that evening. (This was the first sign that he might be moving on.) We continued to wait, and after several more months, the stalker lost interest in this particular couple.

It should be noted that nothing was changed in the security arrangements for these individuals, and the restraining order is still in effect with the same attention from law enforcement. This is just one of those situations in which the natural course of time, and the stalker's seeming to find other interests, diffused the situation naturally. This does not mean that he is positively gone forever, but it is a positive sign that such is the case. This is a situation in which any more overt contact with the stalker would have probably exacerbated the situation, subjecting the victims to a tremendously more traumatic course of events than they ultimately experienced.

However, if you wonder if this guy is still out there, I would have to conclude that he is, but the solution sought was for my clients, not the rest of society.

> **•This is a case where serious physical danger was perceived to exist. Law Enforcement and personal security measures were taken, but no direct contact was made with the stalker, and ultimately, the situation diffused itself.**

In another scenario, a victim was being stalked by an individual. This person chose to employ a series of challenges to the victim in the courts. While she defended all the charges brought before the courts alleging some wrongdoing on her part, the mental and financial burden was overwhelming. The irony was that the stalker had left the area and was orchestrating his attacks through unscrupulous attorneys that he was dealing with from several states away.

During the course of defending her, it was determined that the stalker had a series of issues with the local courts, which would create a serious financial burden on him should he be apprehended in the jurisdiction. After the appropriate research on his situation, contacts with the appropriate authorities, and the dispensing of numerous copies of the warrants for his arrest, his attorney was made aware that there were many organizations looking for him should he return to the jurisdiction.

This process was successful for a while, until one day a private investigator contacted the victim's family using a false scenario, attempting to obtain information about the whereabouts of the victim. The victim's sister convinced the investigator to fax some information to them and that she would have her sister (the victim) contact him. That information, provided immediately to me, was adequate to contact the district attorney in the location in which the private investigator was located. The local DA took interest in the fact that this PI was attempting to locate an individual who was in possession of a restraining order issued in her home state. They agreed to investigate and found that the PI was a friend of the stalker. The PI was prosecuted for his actions in his own jurisdiction.

•Again, no direct contact was made with the stalker, but he learned two things: first, that he couldn't come home, and second, that his actions had caused a friend, who had done him a favor, to face the courts for his actions on behalf of the stalker. These were the two actions that ultimately stopped the activities of the stalker. He didn't know who, but he knew that

someone was working with the victim and that his actions were now under a magnifying glass.

In another scenario, the victim was being harassed by an individual who had been an employee of hers. Somewhere along the way, he had developed the belief that there was some degree of personal romantic relationship between him and the victim. By the time the victim retained help in dealing with the situation, she was in an extremely fragile psychological state, and as a result of her condition, compounded with her fear and frustration, she had completely destroyed her credibility with the local authorities.

The stalker was an individual with a violent history and had been a suspect in several violent situations, including a homicide. The location of all this activity was in an extremely rural setting in the mountains of a mid-Atlantic state, and the stalker was a true "mountain man."

After a considerable amount of time had been expended rebuilding the victim's stature with the local authorities, and after accompanying her to any court appearance or other situation in which she could be seen by the stalker, the authorities concluded that it was time to attempt an apprehension of the stalker during one of his bad acts.

On a very cold, winter night, on a rural road, in the middle of the mountains, the stalker was observed by four state troopers, dressed in "camo" attire, waiting in the woods to observe the victim's residence. As the stalker approached, he was confronted. After some questioning, a determination was made that he would be placed under arrest and taken into custody. He was advised of what was to occur, to which he replied that he did not intend to go with them. At that moment, he was offered the opportunity to do things the easy way or the hard way, and he chose the hard way. The result was predictable, and the charges filed not only included those resulting from his stalking activities and a parole violation, but also resisting arrest and assault on four state troopers, all of which netted the stalker about four to seven years as a guest of the state.

> •**This is an example of a situation in which all indirect methods of dealing with the stalker were unsuccessful. The only method that provided any results was that of involving the authorities and, through their actions, putting the stalker's violent tendencies on record and prosecuting him for his acts.**

As we have discussed, every situation is different; things that may be successful in one situation may fail in another. Obviously, the optimum result is to dissuade the stalker by the defensive actions of the victim, with no involvement by anyone else, but that is the ideal. Unfortunately, most cases involving an adversary who is serious about his intentions requires more activity to overcome his plans. But it is generally agreed, by most of those who work in these situations, that as little involvement of others to achieve the objective is normally the most effective solution.

Obviously, that is the purpose of this book: to provide information that will help a reader identify the problem, attempt to quantify the seriousness of the problem, and have a general idea of what can be done to provide assistance.

No author's words will solve every situation, but no one has the slightest chance of success without understanding her predicament. This is what we have tried to do with this book.

CHAPTER 19
DOES IT EVER END?

"I am the Master of my fate; I am the Captain of my soul."
—from "Invictus" by William Ernest Henley

There is what I believe to be a very good reason for the reference to this poetry in the beginning of this book and now as we again make reference to it at the end of our journey. Since we're near the end, this might be a good time to go back to the beginning and reread Henley's words. I know that there are a variety of interpretations about Henley's meanings, but I believe that his words have special meaning to those whose lives are in a state of turmoil and trauma. If you've been paying attention throughout the pages of this book, you should have picked up on a prevailing theme— that **IT IS ALL ABOUT YOU!** It is about your ability to reach into the depths of your being and pull to the surface that bit of you that says in your heart of hearts you will not be beaten ... you will not be denied your safety, your security, your sanity, your freedom, and your pursuit of happiness.

Does this ever end is a relative question. Will the overt activities against you either stop on their own or be stopped through your own actions to protect yourself? Yes, and in almost all cases this occurs. However, when we consider whether all of this ever ends in your mind, the answer is no. Memories of this experience will always be with you, which isn't necessarily all bad. Memories of the trauma that you have experienced can be extremely beneficial in helping you to avoid future excursions into harm's way. While the

127

memory of all this will never be a positive in your vault of cherished thoughts, how you are able to deal with the recollections of these experiences will determine whether your recollections are positive or negative.

In the course of my daily business contacts, while explaining the range of issues that I normally handle, it is not unusual when I mention these types of cases that someone in the room will say something like, "I wish that I would have known about you when I had my problem," or "I went through something like that." In the course of writing this book, there have been numerous individuals who have seen me writing on airplanes or in airports and struck up conversations. Again, it is not unusual for someone to begin relating her own experience. No one ever forgets.

Your goal should be to season the memory of all this with an understanding that your life will go on, better than it was before, because you will never again be controlled beyond the degree of what you have learned is reasonable, appropriate, healthy, and safe. You will have friends, you will have relationships, you will have all the things that you once had, but so long as you choose not to, you will not become a victim.

Now, this isn't to say that because of your past experiences, you will never again be able to have a meaningful relationship. I am merely saying that when a relationship possibility occurs and begins to develop, you will be able to read the danger signs, hopefully, much better than you could in the past. If you choose to ignore them, then you probably need to skip right on back to the chapter on "exit strategies," reread it, and brush up on your plan … for you will, no doubt, be needing it again someday.

I would not say to you that you may never be accosted by an individual who has found you to be the object of his obsession, for we all know that your personality probably makes you attractive to others. But let us hope that if that ever happens to you in the future, you will be able to immediately recognize the signs and either extricate yourself or seek the proper help.

I would never begin to suggest that just because you have successfully handled a situation with a previous partner that there will be no reoccurrence. But hopefully, you will realize that there are measures that you can take to "level the playing field."

Our friend Henley makes a variety of valid points in "Invictus," and as you read through his words, remember one important fact: He in no way speaks to issues such as wealth, position, or circumstances of situation. He speaks merely of the human spirit.

As I have told you many times in the previous pages, it's all about you and your ability to refuse to be beaten. I wouldn't say that you couldn't be helped by someone even if you weren't maintaining such a posture, but the chances of success are overwhelmingly greater when you have the conviction that you will not be beaten, and the chance of slipping back into the same problem, either with the same person or another like him, is greatly reduced when you have the commitment to win this war.

Henley describes not only the conviction to overcome, but the ability to recognize the crisis, describing the depths of darkness and despair and the punishments to come. He talks of unrelenting resistance against failure, driven by the ultimate belief that YOU are the "Captain." I've always felt that his words were an inspiration to anyone who was wrestling with overwhelming problems in his or her life. Maybe you, too, will find meaning in those words.

No one has, nor will anyone ever, write a book that can miraculously transform you from a person at risk, living your life in harm's way, to a person capable of carrying on with her life, void of risk, with strength and confidence.

I am no exception to that rule. I have not intended to give you all the solutions to the situations in which you may find yourself, but I am optimistic that I have provided some degree of hope that you can survive all of this. I believe that one of the most distressing facts to be encountered when a person in my field enters cases such as these is the existence of overwhelming despair on the part of the victims, despair that they are trapped with no way out.

If I have done nothing else with this book, I hope that I have convinced you that there is a way out. It may not be easy, it may not be short, it may not be without cost, and it may not be without developing a somewhat different "you" before it all ends. When discouragement begins to overwhelm you over the depth of the hole in which you find yourself, just remind yourself how long it took you to dig that hole and understand that your ascent from the depths of aggravation, fear, panic, and general annoyance is probably proportional. You didn't get there overnight, and you won't get out overnight.

As many have experienced crisis in their lives, some personal and some circumstances of their careers, they have found the strength to overcome their adversaries from a variety of ways. If you're fortunate enough to possess the mental conviction to work methodically through crisis, fear, and danger on your own, you are indeed a fortunate individual. However, there is no shame in needing and asking for help. Sometimes that help can come from places that are least expected (friends, co-workers, or family), and other times it can come from where you would most expect (professional sources). What you should realize though is this: Wherever your help comes from, deep in your own resolve or from others, you must be good to you!

Some things age well, but your well-being is not a block of cheese or a bottle of wine. When you first are able to say to yourself that you may have a problem, you are probably one-half to two-thirds down toward the bottom of the hole. Even though you are the closest to the situation, you are usually the last to recognize and accept the realities of your predicament ... so, time is short. Your adversary has a big lead on you, for he has been in operation for some time now, and you have to get in the game to begin undoing his scheme and returning control of your life to its rightful owner, YOU!

So, someplace between a pamphlet and *War and Peace*, I have tried to give you some insight into those things that I believe would be of assistance to you. I hope that I have succeeded. No one deserves to live in fear, shame, or despair; no one deserves to live life in harm's way; and no one should have her life controlled by anyone but herself.

As I take my leave from you, go with me back to that nightclub so many years ago. Sit at the table with a group of young, scared, undercover state troopers facing the most dangerous assignment in their young lives and careers. Sit there at the table and listen to the words of the "Old Man," the boss, as he speaks deliberately, solemnly, and quietly to us about the task at hand. Listen as he speaks those words that would carry all of us through what was about to come our way, and listen to the words that have been indelibly etched in each of our minds since that night so long ago. Listen to the words that have sustained each of us since that very night. Listen to those words as though he were saying them to you at this very moment …

and …

DON'T LET THE BASTARDS BEAT YOU!

EPILOGUE

As you have wandered through the words of this book, you have been exposed to the experience gained in years of dealing with victims of abusive behavior. While I sincerely hope that this book has provided some degree of help to those of you who are unfortunate enough to be involved in a crisis situation, these words are intended to help you understand what you are experiencing and what type of action might be available and what action you should consider. This book is not a how-to-fix-it manual for stalking.

If your situation is either in its infancy or your opponent is not particularly dangerous or dedicated, you have been exposed to some forms of action that may be helpful, but for most cases, you will need to seek other assistance.

This book is not intended to be a giant infomercial; however, this is what we do at my company, **Joe Rice & Associates.**

It would be wonderful if no one ever needed help for one of these situations, but we all know that the world isn't that easy. So, if we can be of help, you know where to find us.

We have developed a process that can guide you through to evaluate your situation and assist you with further actions to help you extricate yourself from harm's way, should that be necessary.
We can be contacted by phone at 1-877-286-2242, or by e-mail at *jrapfa@msn.com.*

About the Author

Joe Rice is the President and principal officer in Joe Rice & Associates, a private investigations and consulting services corporation.

Significant in his unique qualifications are over 30 years of nationwide criminal, corporate and private client investigative experience; which has afforded him a variety of legal, political and law enforcement contacts.

His extensive background includes law enforcement at the state level, state and federal regulatory interpretation and resolution, executive and personal protection, facilities protection and crisis management. Along with that experience he's developed extensive contacts with prominent clinicians in the psychological field.

Printed in the United States
20941LVS00002B/1-96